THE PRICE OF *LIBERTY*

Rosemary Thomson

"Eternal vigilance is the price of liberty."
—John Philpot Curran

D1616252

Creation House
Carol Stream, Illinois

Published by Creation House, 499 Gundersen Drive,
Carol Stream, Illinois 60187
Library of Congress Card Catalog No. 78-59992
ISBN 0-88419-183-4
Printed in the United States of America

Contents

Foreword

Today, the American family is threatened by a combination of special interests that see government as the only valid, permanent social unit. While the family loses importance under this assault, the state will take its place as the guardian and educator of children. Society will no longer consist of families each with limited autonomy, but will be one vast unit which controls the whole life of each person from cradle to grave. The destruction of the family is the indispensable condition for the realization of the absolute state. Already we see the many ways in which the state gains power as the vitality of the family declines.

It is fitting, therefore, that so many American women now should declare the inalienable right of the family against the claims of the absolute state. They reject the proposition that the whole of human life be reduced to the artificial order of bureaucracy and politics and oppose those who seek to reduce the family to a series of legal relationships between so-called liberated men, liberated women, and liberated children. These women call on us to remember that the rights and duties of the family are independent of government and have been ordained by the Author of all our liberties.

Experience tells us that those who will not learn from history are condemned to repeat it. Does not history tell us that the classical cultures of the ancient world lost their vitality and declined by accepting practices which violate the laws of nature and reason and which deny human dignity? Practices now openly promoted in America today?

The historian Polybius pointed to the aversion to marriage and the family, the practices of homosexuality, infanticide and abortion as the main causes of the decline of ancient Greece. Polybius saw clearly that a nation's moral strength

5

was its real strength. We must ask ourselves whether America is not threatened with a similar destruction.

The only alternative to this social suicide is a national spiritual rebirth and the restoration of the moral dignity of the individual and of the family in which it develops. The family is the first school in which those personal and social virtues, so important to the survival of any society, are taught.

At no time has this been more clear to me than during the two days of ad hoc congressional hearings into the activities of International Women's Year which I sponsored in 1977. I was deeply impressed with the testimony of housewives, mothers, elected officials, officials of the Democratic and Republican parties, lawyers and professors. Here I first met Rosemary Thomson and learned of the IWY Citizens' Review Committee's fight to enable the voice of the majority of American women to be heard.

In *The Price of LIBerty*, Mrs. Thomson recounts her testimony which had such a profound effect on my colleagues at the ad hoc hearings and on many other groups. It is a valuable reference for those seeking to understand what is happening to American family life.

Jesse A. Helms
United States Senator
from North Carolina

Acknowledgments

The Price of LIBerty is the story of God's women and their efforts to preserve America's traditional moral and spiritual values. It is the story of a Great Awakening—perhaps not too unlike the important revivals of history.

This book is dedicated to those hundreds of wives, mothers and career women across the U.S. with whom I have worked and prayed—many of whom I know personally, and others whom I know by phone or letter.

Two women who have truly "denied themselves for Christ's sake" deserve special recognition:

Phyllis Schlafly—whose untiring dedication to God, home and country has inspired thousands, and whose leadership is responsible for raising up God-fearing Christian and Jewish women to defend our faiths and our families;

Marilyn Risinger—my "co-pilot" on speaking trips, my ad hoc "secretary" and midnight typist who always thinks of a way to say "yes" whenever I need a friend.

If, as Phyllis Schlafly's husband, Fred, once told me, "Our families are earning 'stars for their crown,' " then my mother will have ample rewards in Heaven for being grandma-on-the-spot when I need to be away from home; so will my husband, Jim, and our two sons who have encouraged me, helped with homemaking chores and endured dozens of repetitious speeches as my traveling companions!

My prayer is that this book will bring honor and glory to the One who has made it all possible—my Living Lord.

Families under Siege

"The happiest moments of my life have been the few which I have passed at home in the bosom of my family."—Thomas Jefferson

The handful of Pro-Family delegates to the National Women's Conference watched in numb silence as lesbians streamed into the galleries of Houston's Coliseum carrying "gay rights" placards, banners and hundreds of bright balloons declaring "We Are Everywhere." Some of the slogans read, "Jesus was a Homosexual," "Lesbians for Wages for Housework," and "I Love this Woman." Others were too obscene to repeat.

We were only three hundred out of nearly two thousand women and a few men elected to represent the views of all American women from each of the fifty states and U.S. territories. A chilling Texas drizzle was falling outside the auditorium that late Sunday afternoon, November 20, 1977, as the

9

National Women's Conference (NWC) prepared to vote on the final of the "Big Three" resolutions—Sexual Preference.

"Dear Lord!" my heart cried out as we watched the display of unity among most of the remaining delegates. They had donned orange armbands to designate lesbian affection or support of this "alternate lifestyle" which the Holy Scripture calls sin. "Open" gays wore buttons proclaiming, "It's fine to be straight, but gay is great," "Warm Fuzzy Dykes," and "Anita Bryant sucks oranges."

I turned to the president of Nurses for Life seated beside me as a member of our Illinois delegation. "I guess my pastor is right when he says, 'If God doesn't judge this nation's immorality, He'll have to apologize to Sodom and Gomorrah,'" I said.

Jo Higgins just shook her head sadly, tears welling up in her eyes. Earlier in the day, abortionists had passed a Reproductive Freedom resolution calling for Federal legislation to allow and finance abortion-on-demand. It included an end to parental consent for teenagers to take the life of an unborn child. Whipped to a frenzy by anti-life speakers, the cheering crowd had ripped down the Pro-Family banner "Give Life a Chance," featuring pictures of happy babies. In its place, these chanting, jeering women had hoisted a sign: "If men could get pregnant, abortion would be sacred."

And late the night before, after the same ecstatic throng had endorsed ratification of the controversial Equal Rights Amendment (ERA), they had snake-danced around the hall in tow of NOW (National Organization for Women) spokesperson, Karen DeCrow.

I felt the tension mount as Jean O'Leary, co-executive director of the National Gay Task Force, stepped to the platform microphone to read the resolution. She received a raucous, standing ovation.

Chairperson Anne Saunier gavelled for quiet.

"Congress, state, and local legislatures should enact legislation to eliminate discrimination on the basis of sexual and affectional preference in areas including, but not limited to employment, housing, public accommodations, credit, public facilities, government funding, and the military,"

Ms. O'Leary said. She was just warming up.

"State legislatures should reform their penal codes or repeal state laws that restrict private sexual behavior between consenting adults.

"State legislatures should enact legislation that would prohibit consideration of sexual or affectional orientation as a factor in any judicial determination of child custody or visitation rights. Rather, child custody cases should be evaluated solely on the merits of which party is the better parent, without regard to that person's sexual and affectional orientation."

The Pro-Plan delegates roared approval. More gavelling by the Chair allowed them to get in place at the eight floor microphones. Not surprisingly, the plot of the International Women's Year Commission to subvert the intent of Congress was working perfectly. Betty Friedan, mother of the modern feminist movement, spoke in favor of the resolution, as did others. When it was time for opposing discussion, the Chair recognized an IWY official who spoke against it only because it might hurt the cause of ratifying the Equal Rights Amendment by the needed three additional states.

Finally Kathryn Nelson, a Pro-Family delegate, was recognized. "It's a matter of moral rights," protested Mrs. Nelson, a resident of Florida where the hotly contested issue of "gay rights" had been defeated by more than two to one in liberal Dade County just months before. "It will destroy the family. Lesbians can never expect to fit into a basic family life. It's against the laws of God."

Catcalls and jeers echoed around the hall. More gavelling.

The question was called. "Passed," the Chair announced.

The Women's Lib "railroad" was moving full-throttle ahead. For many minutes, lesbian women demonstrated for the news media, hugging and kissing to the revulsion of Christians seated on the floor and observers in the galleries.

Above the commotion, a whistle blown by Pro-Family floor leader Joan Gubbins, an Indiana state senator, signaled our protest. We stood, turning our backs on the podium and on the immoral action perpetrated by the International Women's Year (IWY) Commission, operating out of the U.S. State Department at a cost to taxpayers of five million dollars!

11

Although the outcome was not unexpected by those of us who had been debating against the ERA with feminists for the last six years, too few Americans had seen it coming. My involvement had turned up amusing as well as heartbreaking confrontations. I remembered one debate with a Women's Libber.

"Your husbands may be more comfortable watching you on the television here in the lobby," the producer had suggested. "Mrs. Thomson and Mrs. Huber..."

"*Ms.* Huber," my opponent corrected.

"Excuse me. Ms. Huber. You can come into the studio," he continued. "You'll be on the air in five minutes."

Sociology professor Huber began her feminist view of women on our call-in TV talk show by declaring, "It is the norm for women to work outside the home today, and men love it."

Out in the lobby, Professor Huber's spouse was explaining to my husband, Jim, that he and his wife had a marriage contract. Each one agreed to do certain homemaking chores on a rotating basis. As he spoke, the first commercial aired. It was a household cleaning product.

"I haven't tried that one," the professor's husband observed. "I'll have to test it next time it's my turn to scrub floors!"

Jim, who has probably helped me scrub more floors in twenty years of marriage than any liberated man, had a difficult time maintaining a straight face.

"How ridiculous," Jim had laughed in the car on the way home. "If you love your wife, why do you need a marriage contract to help out around the house! Professor Huber and her husband are grandparents and old enough to know better."

But Women's Lib is not a laughing matter. It steamrolled into the '70s leaving in its wake burned bras, church veils and, sometimes, husbands. (One IWY delegate bragged that she felt wonderful after divorcing her husband to come to the NWC.) It was largely ignored by Christians, tolerantly joked about by average citizens and quickly endorsed by intellectuals, educators, politicians who fancied expedient vote-getting, and the hierarchy of most church bodies and secular organizations.

On the surface the women's movement championed equal pay for women and personal fulfillment. Who could argue with that? And what young mother, wearied of diapers, toy-strewn floors, and lack of money did not read *The Feminine Mystique* in the '60s and exclaim, "Betty Friedan understands me!" What middle-aged housewife, bored with an empty nest, did not theorize, "Liberation must be the answer!" Almost everyone not firmly grounded in Biblical principles, embraced the notion that women were oppressed by the facts of life, society and even the church.

Without investigating the real motives of Women's Lib, Federal and state governments dutifully doled out public funds to establish commissions on the status of women. Then, instead of appointing ordinary homemakers and working women to assess their own concerns, female executives in government and politics were named. When the goals of the U.S. Commission were presented to President Nixon in 1970, it was evident that the attack on family life and the traditional moral values of America's spiritual heritage had begun.

The little-heralded report recommended the need for a slowdown in population growth. And it opposed any modification of the proposed Equal Rights Amendment which would exempt women from military combat, and proposed child development programs.[1] Educators across the land, like Huber, promoted these notions to thousands of university students.

In an interview with *U.S. News and World Report*,[2] Ms. Huber expounded on how liberated women are changing American life: "The fact that the wife is expected to work has all kinds of consequences because it makes her independent of her husband. The divorce rate will increase, as will childless marriages. Some of my students perceive that children [are] economic liabilities. . .a couple can have a really smashing life if they don't take mamma out of the labor market to rear the kids."

"Can government help parents with children?" the interviewer inquired.

"We could extend the kindergarten system down to age one or two. Government could spread the economic burden of rearing children. . .the present system confines little children

13

to the biological parents who. . .produce them. . .it's unplanned and unpredictable. What we have is a kind of slave society. Men take it as their right that there is a class of creature called women who exist basically to serve them. . .If I were a man, I would think twice about changing a world where I had a nice, soft, warm creature trained to treat me with tender loving care, to change my baby's diaper, to watch the kid lest it be creamed by a fire truck, and to do all the things that aren't so much fun while I went off and had a zesty life in the world of work."

For the last ten years, Women's Lib has fed American females this steady diet through education, women's magazines, television and movies: Women must work outside the home for pay, wives should be economically independent, divorce and "living together" are acceptable. Children are burdensome so the Planned Parenthood Association teaches population control through contraceptives or abortion. ("We want Planned Parenthood to teach sex education in all schools, but we're having trouble with some parents," complains Karen DeCrow.)

Not until pro-feminist legislators began introducing and sometimes passing laws which put their proposals into practice did the attack on the family become sobering. The Child Development Act was passed by Congress in 1971, to provide "comprehensive" day care for children of all socio-racial-economic backgrounds. President Nixon vetoed the bill charging that it favored "communal modes of child-rearing as against the family-centered approach."[3]

But government child-rearing advocates did not give up easily. In 1975, Sen. Walter Mondale—now Vice President—co-sponsored the Child and Family Services Act. Proponents declared "it is essential" that child rearing begin at age three by a "partnership" of Federal, state, local governments, and parents and community agencies!

When I secured a copy of the bill through my Congressman's office, I was amazed to see that elected government officials were parroting the philosophy of the militant National Organization for Women founded by Betty Friedan. In their policy manual, *Revolution: Tomorrow is NOW*,[4] demands

14

are made for Federal and state governments to set up child care centers for children of all ages. These centers are not simply to care for children whose mothers must work, but would provide developmental care: nutritional, medical, physical, emotional and educational. The difference was that Mondale's bill would require a fee based on the parents' ability to pay, while NOW wants the centers free like libraries, parks, schools and playgrounds. Either way, our pre-school children's mentor becomes our "Father" in Washington, D.C.!

As I sat through the long hours of the National Women's Conference that weekend of November 19-21, 1977, one thing became very clear to me. The national leaders of the women's movement, who were working so hard to ratify ERA, were the same clique promoting homosexual rights, abortion, and government child rearing. The Child Care Resolution passed by the NWC reads in part, "The Federal government should assume a *major* role in directing and providing comprehensive, voluntary, flexible hour, bias-free, non-sexist, quality child care and developmental programs....Labor and management should be encouraged to negotiate child care programs in their collective bargaining agreements."[5]

This "right of all mothers to quality child care," as one Pro-Plan delegate put it, would cost twenty-five billion in Federal taxes annually.[6] But when a Pro-Family woman managed to get to a microphone to ask what this resolution would cost, the Chair replied, "That is not relevant. You are out of order!"

Why the need for such all-encompassing child rearing centers which, in the words of Ms. Friedan, are "staffed by licensed practical mothers of both sexes?" (Would the staffs, perhaps, be like the one which provided child care for Hawaii's IWY meetings—the "gay" community?) As one AP story, titled "Working Wives Happier," whined: "The housewives expend great effort but don't get recognition for it. Their husbands accuse them of 'doing nothing all day' and in the next breath remind them that their duty is to stay home and keep house. A job takes a woman out of the home and the regular paycheck is proof of work well done."

In fact, proponents of the Equal Rights Amendment claim women are "second-class citizens," and that the Constitution does not even recognize women as persons! No wonder a small-town young mother grabbed me by my hand when I finished speaking on the Scripture's value of homemakers.

"I'm so thrilled to hear you say that," she said. "All of my friends have gone back to work, and they're making me feel guilty because I enjoy staying at home just taking care of my husband and kids."

Pediatrician Robert S. Mendelsohn, who was medical consultant for Project Head Start, questions whether the American family can survive: "The quest for 'self-fulfillment' has relegated the family to second-class status and has given us a sky-rocketing divorce rate, national abortion rate of 615,800 in 1973 [one million in 1977] and a workforce of millions of women who think that society doesn't value them unless they are gainfully employed."[7]

King Solomon's wisdom is as timely as in Old Testament days: "Every wise woman buildeth her house; but the foolish plucketh it down with her own hands."

Yet that is exactly what Women's Lib is all about. Under the guise of "equal rights" the feminists are systematically plucking down their own house both literally and figuratively. The remaining twenty-two resolutions, passed as the National Plan of Action at the National Women's Conference, are an attempt to coerce Congress into passing laws that would dismantle America's free-enterprise system under which our diverse religious faiths and families have had liberty to flourish and grow.

So drastic are some of the proposals that a Georgia IWY official—once national secretary of NOW and a former ERA supporter—wrote President Carter: "The thrust of the recommendations is towards greater dependence on government—primarily Federal. . .there is a trend towards transforming family relationships into employment relationships which would adapt to monetary equations for computing the Gross National Product!. . .I urge you to look askance at proposals to place a dollar value on family relationships and on all recommendations which flow in the direction of governments restructuring society rather than society restructuring governments."

Examples of this thinking were the "Wages for Housework" signs at the NWC. When a Washington, D.C., reporter inquired at one such booth in the Houston exhibit hall just how much housewives should be paid annually, the reply was $20,000.

"When I note that 40 million women are housewives," the newsman wrote, "which means that her proposal would cost a mere $800 billion annually, and ask who will pay these salaries, she is obviously bored with such details. . . .Well, there are 'profits from corporations and money within the government,' she says."

To make housewives "economically independent," IWY's Homemakers Resolution urged "Congress [to] support a practical plan for covering homemakers in their own right under social security"—no longer under their husband's account. Unveiled by HEW in April 1978, this plan to improve social security benefits for women would have homemakers paying social security taxes on their supposed worth into their own account.

A *Redbook* survey inadvertently exposed the feminist philosophy of independence from a husband, noting that the greater a woman's religious convictions, the more likely she is to be satisfied with her marital relationship, more likely to describe it as "very, very good." The fundamental difference that distinguished the non-religious from the strongly religious woman is that the non-religious woman is far more likely to be dissatisfied with every aspect of life. By a striking margin she is less likely to describe herself as "happy most of the time," less likely to rate her marriage as "very good."[8]

The popular assertion that women's roles are changing has instead become, for Christians, the burning question, *who is changing women's roles?*

How often the Bible warns, "be not deceived." The plain fact is that women are being promised "liberation" from the plan God established for the family. The price of LIBerty may be as costly as the one paid by our "foremother" in the Garden of Eden.

The Most Innocent Victim

"Thus saith the Lord that made thee, and formed thee from the womb."—Isaiah 44:2

The Lord certainly works in mysterious ways. As I and the other three downstate delegates waited to make our connection at bustling O'Hare International Airport, who should join the line for boarding the same plane home but our own Congressman.

"How did your conference go, girls?" he boomed in his jovial manner.

Exhausted from lack of sleep, discouraged by the atmosphere of the National Women's Conference, we groaned in unison. The timing was perfect for giving him a firsthand report of the atrocities committed over the weekend in the name of "women's rights."

"They voted for more Federal funding and control of every area of our lives from the cradle to the grave. . .*if* you can make it to the cradle," one of our ladies quipped.

The declaration of war against the most helpless member of the family—the unborn child—had been announced by the U.S. Supreme Court in January 1973. My husband and I listened intently from the balcony of McCormick Place's Arie Crown Theatre as Dr. Francis Schaeffer, founder of Switzerland's world-famous L'Abri, traced the history of abortion back to the beginning of the Christian era. Early believers, he said, considered abortion such an offense that any who procured them or made drugs to further them were barred from the Lord's Supper for ten years. On stage at the Chicago premier of his book and film, *How Should We Then Live?*,[1] Schaeffer predicted, "If our culture survives, we will look back to the present abortion climate with as much horror as we now perceive slavery and the Nazi gas chambers."

The historic Supreme Court edict made abortion, for any reason, legal during the first three months, and for many capricious reasons during the remainder of the pregancy. In making his decision, one Justice wrote: "There was no ban on abortion in ancient religions." Since Christianity and Judaism *did* revere the life of pre-born children, he apparently was referring to the pagan phallic cults!

The results of easy abortion, often paid for with our own tax dollars through Federal medical programs, have snowballed. Presumably, the 1973 ruling was meant to prevent back alley butchers from preying upon poor women in trouble. But the record shows otherwise. In one populous Midwest state the Family Planning Council reported that abortion is now a prime factor in birth control.[2] More than half are performed on white women, not poor minorities.

Dr. Louis Keith, of Northwestern University Medical School, terms the growing dependence on abortion for birth control "disastrous. . . .We didn't realize, and I don't think anybody realizes, how important abortion has become."

In spite of Congressman Henry Hyde's (R.-Ill.) valiant efforts to preserve life by Federal law, the nihilistic attitude is national in scope, at least on the part of so-called experts.

President Carter's task force on alternatives to abortion wrote that the only real alternatives are "suicide, motherhood, and, some would add, madness."

Sitting at a neighborhood gathering recently, I listened as one kaffeeklatscher expounded on the virtues of abortion. Finally, a young mother turned to the speaker.

"We have two adopted children," she said quietly. "We got them before 1973, but my friend who cannot have children of her own either, is now years down the waiting list for an adoptive baby."

The anti-life advocates begin their indoctrinations early. Our son's Junior High "health" book is a perfect example. Included in the unit on Human Sexuality is a section on "family planning." The authors suggest that the solution to an unwanted child is abortion.[3] There is no indication that it is anything more than a medical procedure or that it has far-reaching moral, religious, or psychological implications. No mention that the unborn child is actually a living human being. No hint of the truth of Psalm 139: "Thou hast covered me in my mother's womb. . . .My substance was not hid from thee, when I was made in secret. . . .Thine eyes did see my substance; yet being unperfect; and in thy book all my members were written, which in continuance were fashioned, when as yet there was none of them."

Have you looked at your child's textbooks lately? Or viewed the film frequently shown in "Family Life" classes by Planned Parenthood? This trend could have been predicted easily by alert Christians as early as 1972. At that time, the prestigious *New York Times* quoted Congresswoman Patsy T. Mink (D.-Hawaii): "Keeping women in the home may be the major contributor to excess population growth. . . .If we encourage policies which will permit women to choose other roles," insisted Ms. Mink who was later to become a member of the International Women's Year Commission, "many will leave the home and thus decide to have fewer children. We should encourage this movement of women into the work force. . . .It is not coincidental that many of the goals of 'Women's Liberation' center on getting out of the traditional home role."[4]

The same *New York Times* supplement, sponsored by the Population Crisis Committee and Planned Parenthood, also carried a Report of the U.S. Commission on Population Growth and the American Future chaired by John D. Rockefeller III. It recommended:

• "The Federal government enact a Population Education Act to assist school systems in establishing well-planned population education programs.

• "In order to neutralize the legal, social and institutional [church] pressures that historically have encouraged childbearing. . .we should eliminate descrimination based on sex by adopting the proposed Equal Rights Amendment.

• "To enable all Americans. . .to avoid unwanted births. . . [we must] liberalize access to abortion services. . ."

On January 23 of the following year, abortion became the law of the land!

All fifteen hundred seats at Grace Presbyterian Church were taken. My husband, along with the other ushers, began setting up folding chairs. It was a packed house as Maria Anne Hirschmann, author of *Hansi, the Girl Who Loved the Swastika*, stepped to the microphone. She began with her customary simple prayer, "Lord make me a nail upon the wall, fastened securely in its place, and on that thing, so insignificant and so very, very small, hang a bright picture of Thy wonderful face."

In her unmistakable German accent, she told of the horrors of the Third Reich; how she had been swept up in its propaganda. Then she said something that jolted us upright in the padded pews: "Don't ever let anyone tell you that abortion does not lead to euthanasia (mercy killing), because that's exactly where it leads. I know—I saw it happen in my native land."

To emphasize the growing anti-life attitude in America, she told us of a mother-to-be who came to her for counseling. In tears, the young woman had told how she had contracted three-day measles during her early weeks of pregnancy. Now her physician and friends were pressuring her to have an abortion because of the risk of delivering a less-than-normal child. After much prayer with Hansi, she decided to put the baby in the Lord's hands. She would not kill her offspring.

"What a thrill it was," Mrs. Hirschmann related, "to get a letter not long ago from the new mother praising God for a perfect, beautiful baby daughter named Hansi!"

My friend, Shirley Bergstrom, was not so lucky as the world counts luck.

"When the nurse brought Stevie in to me for the first time, I sensed something was wrong," she remembers. "It wasn't until the pediatrician checked over our only son a few days later that my worst fears were confirmed."

"I believe your baby has Down's Syndrome," the doctor said soberly.

"The Lord has taught us the real meaning of love these past twelve years through Steve," Shirley relates. "Most people pray and read God's Word to become more loving; with Steve it's just there. If you hurt, he hurts. If he gets something, he always wants to share with his sisters. He has such a loving spirit that he never fights or whines over 'who got the most' like many kids."

This loving spirit has spilled over into his two sisters' lives. Ten-year-old Dawn is philosophical about Steve.

"My brother has a disability of learning. It just takes him longer to learn," she says with a shrug. "I wouldn't want to trade him for anybody else. I wouldn't want anything to happen to him either."

At seventeen, Debbie's spiritual maturity shows in the way she thinks about her brother. "I used to get a sick feeling inside everytime I heard someone call anybody 'retarded' or make fun of a person who was. I felt like screaming at them, 'You don't even know what it means to be retarded!' But God took that feeling away," she says. "He made me realize that those kids were just talking off the tops of their heads. If they knew my brother, Steve, they would think differently.

"The Lord knew what He was doing when He gave us Steve. The Bible says that God will not give us more than we can handle (I Corinthians 10:13). And although Steve is a slow learner, the joy he brings to our family is more than words can say! Sometimes he is so forgiving and loving it makes me ashamed of myself. I know one thing for sure—I would never

22

want to trade my brother for any other brother in the world!"

Only the year before Steve's birth, Shirley had totally committed her life to Christ as Lord and Savior. Naturally, she cried when she learned the truth. But there was no doubt the Lord had given Steve to them for a reason, and she had peace about her son.

"Oh, at first, I worried a little how he would get along," she says. But her fears soon were erased. "You just can't feel sorry for a guy who is so happy all the time. Wherever we go, he makes friends. He remembers people by name, and everyone likes to hear his name. So you see, he has many qualities that most people strive for but few ever achieve!

"Yes, I know there are tests today that tell you if the baby has Down's Syndrome before it is born. But think what a blessing we'd have missed if I had known and had an abortion," Shirley maintains.

Yet, agitation by the women's movement for "reproductive freedom" has reached a crescendo. The original IWY Commission voted 33-2 in favor of Federally financed abortion. Serving on IWY's Reproductive Freedom Committee was a member of Planned Parenthood — but no member of Right to Life. The basis for this committee's abortion recommendation came from the Religious Coalition for Abortion Rights:[5] "When talking about abortion, one must distinguish between the morality of action and the morality of a law about that action. The rightness or wrongness of an abortion, per se, is not the same as the rightness or wrongness of a law that would prohibit abortion altogether. One might believe that abortion is wrong, and at the same time, maintain that laws prohibiting abortion also are wrong, without being morally inconsistent."

In my many debates with feminists, I answer this twisted rationale with this statement: "You mean that while you yourself would not commit murder, it's all right for someone else to do it?"

Significantly, eighteen months after Dr. Bernard Nathanson opened the first legal abortion clinic in New York state, he resigned, saying, "I became convinced that as director of the clinic I had, in fact, presided over 60,000 deaths."[6]

"We have lost more lives to abortion than in all the wars and traffic accidents in the history of the United States. Does the abortionist become more ethical," asks Dr. Bruce W. Dunn of the "Grace Worship Hour" (Channel 13, Peoria, Illinois), "by moving him from the back alley to the Main Street Clinic?"

And Hansi's predictions may become a striking reality, according to an account of a Women's Lib speech, "From Abortion on Demand to Post Birth Termination," reported in the *National Right To Life News,* July 1977.

"Being courageous isn't easy," the feminist said. "I've always been out in front on all the big issues. I mean, ten years ago. . .I was marching for abortion on demand. Now I'm in the forefront of this great struggle—infanticide on demand." She paused to let the shock sink in. . .

"Look, abortion on demand is universally accepted. School girls can get abortions without parental consent. (Supreme Court ruling, July 1, 1976.) Nobody fights abortion anymore. Nobody important, anyway. . . .Infanticide on demand is merely the next progressive stage after abortion in the struggle for a truly humane society. If it's okay to kill, uh, I mean terminate a month-old fetus, why isn't it okay to terminate a month-old baby? What is the difference?"

Come to think of it (wrote the reporter) no difference at all, you had to admit!

"The door is open," warns Dr. Schaeffer. "The courts have arbitrarily separated 'aliveness' from 'personhood.' And if this is so, why not arbitrarily do the same with the aged?. . .If the majority vote supported it, it would become 'right' to kill the old, the incurably ill, the insane. And other groups could be declared non-persons. No voice could be raised against it."

A prominent British physician currently advocates euthanasia for the elderly, and Dr. C. Everett Koop, chief of surgical services at Children's Hospital, Philadelphia, worries that infanticide is being practiced right now in this country "by that very segment of our profession which has always stood in the role of advocate for the lives of children. . . .I am concerned that there is no outcry, because when the first 273,000 German aged, infirm and retarded were killed in gas chambers, there

24

was no outcry from that medical profession either, and it was not far from there to Auschwitz."

Whenever I debate the Equal Rights Amendment, my opponents invariably deny that it will have any effect on abortion even though Betty Friedan said, "As for reliance on future Supreme Courts—that is the reason we need ERA."

Senator Joan Gubbins shared a letter with me that was received by a colleague in the Indiana Senate from Law Professor Charles E. Rice of Notre Dame. "You asked my opinion as to the possible effect of the Equal Rights Amendment on state laws restricting abortion," he wrote. "If ERA were adopted, it would make clear beyond any doubt that the states would be disabled from prohibiting or even restricting abortion in any significant way. Abortion is an operation which can be performed only upon women. The combination of the Supreme Court abortion decisions and the ERA would operate to prevent any restrictions on abortion which are more stringent than the restrictions imposed on sexually neutral operations such as appendectomies. In fact, I believe that the adoption of the ERA would jeopardize...the so-called conscience clauses which give medical personnel the right to refuse on grounds of conscience to perform abortions."

Already, some American medical schools discriminate against a prospective student if he or she opposes abortion, and Senator Richard Schweiker's (R.-Pa.) bill prohibiting exclusion of Pro-Life students has been derailed.

Diminutive Pepper Root of Columbus, Ohio, is a classic answer to the feminists' claim that pre-born children are not "viable" persons. Only a half-term baby, Pepper weighed-in at one pound, six ounces when she was born April 27, 1976. Eighteen months later her pediatrician reported the tot growing at a perfectly normal rate with good eyesight and no evidence of brain damage.[7]

"I feel we have been blessed so much!" says her mother.

Nevertheless, Women's Lib will carry its Reproductive Freedom demand to President Carter and Congress this year in the form of the National Women's Conference Plan of Action—supposedly representing the majority of American women. As NOW officials Karen DeCrow and Eleanor Smeal (also an IWY Commissioner and member of the newly appointed National Advisory Commitee for Women, 1978) pointed out on the "Phil Donahue Show," "You can't be a feminist without being in favor of abortion."[8]

There is much Scriptural truth in the popular squibb on feminism:

> Adam's rib,
> Satan's fib,
> Life of trib,
> Mary's sib,
> Women's lib,
> Females glib,
> Empty crib!

Goodby, Little Red Schoolhouse

"Train up a child in the way he should go..."
—Proverbs 22:6

Twelve-year-old Craig stormed into our kitchen. Throwing his school books on a chair, he exploded, "I'm going to write my Congressman! The music teacher says we can't have our Junior High boys' chorus next year. Some stupid government rules. We have to call it the 'changing voices' chorus and let girls in!"

Another pre-teen, who lives halfway across the country from Craig, was equally miffed when the Wethersfield, Connecticut, schools fell victim to the women's movement and Federal sex discrimination guidelines, disbanding their all-boy choir rather than risk losing $70,000 in Federal aid.

"Women's Liberation?" says Emerson Kellogg III in disgust.

27

"I think it stinks."

However, Title IX Guidelines of the 1972 Education Act are applauded by feminists. They are a forecast of ERA's uni-sex society envisioned by Women's Lib. Former secretary of HEW, Casper Weinberger, had to "plead to grant a special exemption for Boy Scouts and Girl Scouts from the broad sweep of the anti-sex discrimination statute."[1] But GSA national board member, Betty Friedan, wants to merge girls and boys into a Human Scout Movement! In fact, HEW's bureaucracy and groups like NOW and IWY—with Girl Scout national president Gloria Scott as a member—all are working together with "progressive" educators to promote dramatic changes in public education. They are succeeding. Christian parents who wonder why they are sometimes losing their children to alien philosophies have not recently investigated textbooks.

I concluded my presentation at the annual STOP ERA Conference and was proceeding back to my seat when a lady in the audience caught my arm.

"Now I know why the Lord sent me to this conference!" she whispered. "You are a writer and I have a story to tell."

Laura Rogers had detected a frightening change in their eighth grader. He had become restless, unable to sleep, burdened with anxiety. She looked for causes in their home. Then evidence of drugs. Finally, she questioned him about his classroom materials. He didn't want to talk about school—especially social studies. Pressed for answers, he admitted that he was studying a "different" kind of story.

"It's about a nigger who gets kicked in the ass," he mumbled, averting his eyes.

"John," she admonished. "How dare you talk like that in our Christian home!" She could hardly believe him, but the pained look on the boy's face told her something was wrong. When Mrs. Rogers secured a copy of the paperbacks used in her son's class, a high school teacher wrote an evaluation.

The books were designed to teach attitudes—not history or social studies. One volume gave a detailed case study of a high school "rebellion" where students took over their school;

another described a 16-year-old boy's "rebellion" against his "mean" father. The "Teacher Tactics Manual" instructed the teacher to "stress that rebellion involves going against a recognized authority." The series used profanity, ethnic and racial insults, tales of personal violence and stories about civil disobedience.

While the texts presented history as a series of class struggles—black vs. white, men vs. women, youth vs. age—huge gaps occurred in chronological history, and important American figures were neglected or ignored. Benjamin Franklin got one short sentence while an entire paragraph was devoted to the American Nazi party. Legalized abortion and marijuana were presented as social accomplishments in the year 2000. And religion was mentioned in a negative manner with Christian ideals being equated with the tenets of the Ku Klux Klan.

Laura Rogers discovered what Texans Mel and Norma Gabler[2] have been fighting for the last ten years—publishers that are rewriting the curriculum to reflect Secular Humanism.[3] Its moral relativism—no absolutes, no right or wrong—has replaced the values of Western Christian culture and basic skills.

Speaking before the Nevada State IWY Conference, national IWY commissioner Gloria Steinem publicly tied Women's Lib to this "new religion." "Feminism leads to humanism and humanism is the goal," she said. Earlier, the *MS.* magazine editor told *Saturday Review of Education,* "By the year 2000 we will, I hope, raise our children to believe in human potential, not God."

Just before the National Women's Conference, we delegates received a news release from IWY chairperson Bella Abzug. Datelined the U.S. State Department and mailed with the government's "free" postage frank, it attacked those who did not support the proposed National Plan of Action, equating us with the Ku Klux Klan. The particularly family-oriented Mormon Church was singled out for special vilification. It was, of course, the 300 Pro-Family delegates—Christians from many denominations who believe the Bible's moral principles—whom Ms. Abzug accused of being extremists.

The lines for the spiritual battle had been drawn: Christians vs. Humanist/Feminists. As the NWC dragged on in the

Coliseum, Pro-Family delegate Bonnie Bowlby asked slyly, "Everyone else is here, but where are the Romans?" We certainly felt as though we had been thrown to the lions!

Interestingly, the demographics of the NWC were not balanced by age.[4] Although the percentage of women in the 25-55 age bracket is 49 percent nationally, the conference's percentage was nearly 78 percent. How had a whole generation been conditioned to reject Judeo-Christian standards? It did not happen overnight and it did not happen by accident.

My first year at a state university, I had the nicest education professor. He was pleasant, helpful; he even invited me to go with his family to their church's Sunday night social. For the life of me, I couldn't understand why campus rumor held that the professor was "pink" (a term from the '50s signifying a leftist). The history of education was fascinating. All my family were teachers, and now I was proud to be learning about John Dewey—the father of progressive education—who began implementing his new teaching techniques in the 1920s.

It was not until I had children of my own that I began reading *all* of Dewey's theories. To my astonishment, I discovered that "progressive education" was a code phrase for using the schools to restructure society!

"I believe," Dewey wrote, "that education is the fundamental method of social progress and reform. . .the only sure method of social reconstruction."[5]

Now fifty years later, Betty Friedan is saying the ultimate goal of the women's movement is to "restructure institutions." Ms. Friedan and John Dewey are both signers of the *Humanist Manifesto*,[6] along with an official of Planned Parenthood and behavioral scientist B.F. Skinner.

The manifesto minces no words defining humanist beliefs and goals: "Humanists still believe that traditional theism, especially faith in the prayer-hearing God. . .is an unproved and outmoded faith. . .diverting people with false hopes of heaven hereafter. Reasonable minds look to other means for survival. . . .We can discover no divine purpose or providence for the human species. . . .No deity will save us; we must save ourselves. . . .Promises of immortal salvation or fear of eternal damnation are both illusory and harmful. . ."

The manifesto goes on to affirm that moral values derive their source from human experience. Ethics is autonomous (do your own thing) and situational. Everyone has the right to abortion, divorce, sexual behavior between consenting adults . . .euthanasia and suicide. In support of a one-world government, humanists "deplore the division of humankind on nationalistic grounds" and work for "the development of. . .a world order based upon transnational federal government" where "extreme disproportions in wealth, income, and economic growth should be reduced on a worldwide basis."

The American Humanist Association was founded in 1933 with John Dewey as a member of its board. Only the year before, Professor Dewey—then head of Columbia University's Teacher's College—expounded: "There is no God and there is no soul. Hence, there is no need for the props of traditional religion. With dogma and creed excluded, then immutable truth is also dead and buried. There is no room for fixed, natural law or permanent moral absolutes."[7]

The newly organized National Education Association (NEA) echoed these sentiments. Evidence that NEA has pursued Dewey's goals up to the present became clear during contract negotiations between our local school board and teachers in the fall of 1976.

With the Illinois Education Association, an NEA affiliate, representing and directing area teachers, they ran a newspaper advertisement attacking the superintendent, and distributed literature based on a publication entitled "Better Educational Standards for Today" (BEST), published by IEA.

My husband and I felt that it was the responsibility of Christian parents to take a stand on behalf of the elected school officials and the administration they had hired.

"We would like to support our school board's contract decision," I told the superintendent by phone. "I am willing to write an advertisement to counteract that misleading one the bargaining group ran in the paper. But I need accurate facts to answer the teachers' complaints."

The educators' ad *sounded* good. The school board was

keeping them from creating a "quality" system. But having had a mother who resigned from the IEA years before because of the association's humanist views, I suspected that their notion of "quality" was quite different from the average parent's. The BEST booklet which the superintendent gave me confirmed my suspicions.

The introduction set the tone: "Implementation of these standards will require drastic changes. . ." It called for a high degree of teacher autonomy, including selecting administrative and teaching staffs, and full authority to decide what to teach and how to teach it. We Christian parents, who are responsible to God for our children, raised an eyebrow at the suggestion that the "proletariat" take over the "factories" of education!

The BEST publication went on, "We live in a highly dynamic world—society and culture change constantly; what was appropriate yesterday is hardly acceptable today. . ." Couched in "educationese," that theory is exactly the same espoused by the *Humanist Manifesto*—no absolutes, no right or wrong!

A BEST teacher is to help children develop appropriate *attitudes*, and recognizes that such values are more easily transmitted in an atmosphere free from censorship and artificial restraints, IEA authors advised. "Like the restraints of the Ten Commandments?" I asked myself.

"Sex role stereotyping" must be eliminated. (This stereotyping is showing the man as the head of the family and the woman as a homemaker and mother!) And a picture of boys engaging in a sport like football while girls watch may traumatize your grade school daughter for life. There should be a "student rights" policy. And guidance counselors need to promote "goal-directed behavior."

Students' rights to have "meaningful" classes—not boring math, English or science—have generated a proliferation of nonacademic courses. Even worse than the steady decline in college entrance test scores is the fact that high school graduates are being turned out into the job market without even minimum competency skills—they can't read, write or do simple arithmetic beyond a 6th grade level. The situation is so bad that parents in various parts of the country are beginning to sue school districts for allowing this to happen to their children.

To top all this, the National Gay Task Force (NGTF) is urging school counselors to present a positive view of homosexuals! Delegates to the National Women's Conference received a letter from Jean O'Leary asking our support of the Sexual Preference Resolution which would allow "open" lesbian and homosexual teachers to become role models for our children. Her idea of "goal-directed behavior" is having lesbians represented on the guidance staff.

"No school counselor should ever refer a student to a psychotherapist for the purposes of changing her/his sexual preference from gay to straight," urges an NGTF position paper co-authored by Ms. O'Leary. "Textbooks which do not mention lesbianism or which refer to it as a mental disorder should not be used. . . .Lesbian clubs should be established in the schools."

The Bible was never more relevant. Peter wrote, "While they promise them liberty, they themselves are servants of corruption!" (II Peter 2:19)

BEST educators say that a teacher should meet the standards established by the respective curricular fields, such as those created by the American Personnel and Guidance Association. Is it coincidence that *A Lesbian Guide*, prepared by the NGTF and, according to a boldface notation on the cover, "Officially Approved by the National Commission on the Observance of International Women's Year," lists the American Personnel and Guidance Association and NEA among organizations that have issued support and policy statements on gay rights!

Not all attempts to mold students are quite so obvious. Several years ago our oldest son was involved in an eighth grade role-playing unit called "Sunshine City." I guessed something was amiss when Scott, not one to discuss details of school, told us at the dinner table one evening, "Mr. Brunswick (not his real name) called me a bigot in class today."

"What?" Jim and I asked incredulously.

"Yeah, I'm supposed to be a WASP. . ."

"A what?"

"WASP—White Anglo Saxon Protestant," he explained. "I'm a member of Sunshine City's School Board and I voted against busing kids across town so schools would be socio-economically-racially balanced. That's when the teacher called me a bigot."

I had read a lot about sensitivity training, a form of behavioral science developed by B.F. Skinner to change attitudes, but I didn't want to believe it was happening in our own community. Why, most people were from strong Bible-believing churches! Reluctantly, I asked Scott to bring his book home. But there was no text for this class, only a xeroxed sheaf of papers from—as I later learned—a major behavioral science center in California. The six-week innovation centered around a hypothetical town where the teacher, posing as God, drew events out of a hat at random. One could not miss the implication that God has no plan or purpose for every life. One typical project was to list the contributions made by Malcolm X.

When Jim and I met with the two teachers of Sunshine City and several members of the administration to express our concern, we were made to feel like meddling nitwits. I was amazed; most of the men attended fundamental churches and Mr. Brunswick was even a minister.

"How can you expect 13-year-olds to find Malcolm X's promotion of rioting and racism a contribution to our society?" I asked.

"Well, contribution doesn't necessarily mean something good," Mr. Brunswick answered defensively.

"I'd have to agree with the Thomsons," the superintendent sided. "The ordinary meaning for contribution is a positive one."

Still, no one really saw that the experimental social studies/language arts unit was a form of attitude changing.

"Things like diagramming sentences are not important anymore," one teacher said. "Whoever diagrams a sentence when he gets out of school?"

I guess that is why most colleges by the late '70s must offer remedial English for many incoming freshmen. It is why *Time* magazine devoted eight pages to its November 14, 1977, cover story on education in the U.S.

"After more than a decade of vaunted 'innovations'—free-form 'open classroom' programs, flexible modular scheduling, enough electronic gadgetry to make some schoolrooms look like Mission Control—all signs indicate that today's students are more poorly equipped in basic skills than were their predecessors," *Time* concluded.

For example, the magazine visited one college-prep English class where the teacher was instructing students how "to talk to one another." She "pouts and gestures to illustrate tone and attitude changes, then reads a short story about being loving and capable. For homework, the students are told to make a tear in a sheet of paper each time someone is mean to them and a pencil mark when someone makes them feel good about themselves. The kids snicker as they file out."

In addition, schools are victims of the "no absolutes" humanist viewpoint. "The mayhem wreaked by students on their own schools," the article states, "continues to grow. In 1975 . . .secondary students attacked 63,000 teachers, pulled off 270,000 burglaries and destroyed school property worth $200 million. The level of violence has continued to climb. . ."

To what did *Time* attribute the current crisis? "John Dewey's ideas about 'progressive' education. . . .Add to the school's problems those of society: more broken homes, more two-income families with no one to mind the children and—not least—less reverence for the written word." It appears that John Dewey is the "father" of Women's Lib, and that Ms. Steinem incorrectly assumed that feminism leads to humanism because it occurred the other way around. Humanistic education produced an entire generation of women without moral absolutes who voted for IWY's National Plan of Action without a second thought. Humanism left a God-shaped vacuum which Women's Lib filled, and placed Man—excuse me, Woman—on the throne demanding "equal rights."

One can almost hear the prophet lamenting down the corridors of time, "All we like sheep have gone astray. We have turned everyone to *her* own way" (Isaiah 53:6).

Coming Up, Brave New World

*"The only thing necessary for evil to succeed is
for good men to do nothing."—Edmund Burke*

I watched the Ozark DC-9 brake to a deafening halt. The
ramp came down, and deplaning passengers hurried into the
terminal. A statuesque blond clutching a bulging briefcase
paused momentarily, then spotted me among the waiting
crowd beyond the security gate.

"How ya' doing!" she puffed, giving me a quick hug.

"Well, I'm glad Indiana's legislature finally adjourned,"
I said. "When did you finish?"

"At 2:00 a.m. today." Senator Joan Gubbins sighed. "But
the spring session was great. My bill to prevent explicit sex
education in schools passed!"

Senator Gubbins, a member of the Education Committee

36

and the Fact-Finding Committee on Sex Education, had taken a leadership role against the influx of Godless humanism in her state's schools since she became the sole woman elected to the legislature in 1968. She had come to Peoria to teach an adult evening session of our church's Vacation Bible School.

Later, as she unpacked her bags at our home, Joan called out, "Before I forget it, Rosemary, here is a copy of an article from the *NEA Journal* that I want you to have."

Published in January 1969, the reprint (simply titled "70's") envisioned educators assuming formal responsibility for children at age two. Its logic was that it is easier to teach behavior or attitudes than it is to change them after a child starts kindergarten. Early childhood specialists should guide toddlers in growth and development, nutrition, mental hygiene, and provide curriculum planning, parent education and community relations.

The professional educators' scope is identical to the Child and Family Services Act, the demands of NOW, the BEST goals, and the Child Care Resolution passed by the IWY National Women's Conference in Houston!

John Dewey's humanist philosophy prevails in long-range NEA planning of the '70s:

• "Educational policy decisions in the 1970s will not only anticipate tomorrow, they probably will help to *create* (original emphasis) it.

• "There will be an *international* consensus as to what is desirable in family life, art, recreation, education, diet, economic policies and government.

• "The *worldwide* status and influence of the female will greatly increase. (The introduction to IWY's National Plan of Action, published by the U.S. State Department, affirms, "We are part of a worldwide movement of women.")

• "Differences in wealth and ownership between haves and have-nots will narrow." (What a subtle call for socialistic redistribution of money and property!)

NEA's brave new world forecasts teachers as "learning clinicians. . .this title intended to convey the idea that schools are becoming 'clinics' whose purpose is to provide individualized psychosocial 'treatment' for the student. . ." and "biochemical therapist/pharmacists, whose services increase as biochemical (drug) therapy and memory improvement chemicals are introduced more widely."

"Why, Joan, this is atrocious! We are in a battle for our children's minds," I exclaimed getting out my file of education clippings. "Some of these things already are happening. Here is one article that estimates 500,000 to 850,000 children are given chemotherapy as an 'enlightened' answer to spanking, and parents are complaining that kids are being drugged in an attempt to make them conform to a more acceptable norm.

"Look at this Early Education Project in Brookline, Massachusetts. It's supposed to be a model for future pre-schoolers because 'a child's most critical learning is done before the age of three.' "

The Senator nodded knowingly.

"And what about the MACOS program?" I asked picking out a magazine tearsheet.

"Exactly on target," she confirmed. "The National Science Foundation, with a Federal grant for curriculum development, encourages open-ended discussions that don't teach values one way or another. Right out of humanism's bag of no moral absolutes."

By the mid-'70s humanist thinking had monopolized the upper echelons of the educational community! NEA's dreams were becoming a nightmare for Christian parents.

Dr. Onalee McGraw gripped the podium and leaned forward intensely. "What has replaced basic education?" she asked delegates to the national STOP ERA/Eagle Forum conference. "What is causing the precipitous deterioration of learning achievement in our schools? Many parents have discovered that the answer to both questions is humanistic education."

Her youthful appearance belied the fact that Mrs. McGraw was the recipient of a doctorate degree and the mother of two youngsters. But she was in clear command of her subject matter as she skillfully added the missing pieces of the puzzle that confronted us. We were from nearly every state of the union, that fall of 1976, but as she cited educational trends, we recognized them from our own communities.

"Humanistic education places all emphasis on the child's social and psychological growth, instead of on the learning of basic reading, writing, thinking, communicating skills, and factual knowledge. It emphasizes the thoughts, beliefs, values, opinions, feelings, and the peer group and family adjustment of the student.

"You must understand that there is a major distinction between 'humane conduct' in the classroom and 'humanistic education.' Its essential thrust is to train students how to make moral and ethical decisions deemed appropriate by the tenets of humanism, and to develop their own autonomous value systems," she explained. "However, in the humanistic frame of reference, values are relative and ethics situational. Children are being taught at school that moral and social beliefs and behavior are not necessarily based upon the Judeo-Christian principles being taught by most families at home. An example is the teaching strategy called by several names— values education, moral education or values clarification."[1]

These titles were new to me. Probably some limited experimentation going on somewhere else, I thought, but worth watching for.

The Monday following the conference, Jim and I, along with several other concerned parents, had a meeting with the Junior High health teachers, principal, and a school board member regarding the teaching of Human Sexuality.

Several weeks earlier, I had stumbled across the fact that this unit—everything anyone ever wanted to know about sex— was being taught without parental knowledge or consent. Not only did the text include the portion implicitly endorsing abortion, but it gave strictly physical information—no hint of traditional religious morals. In addition, homosexuality was treated as an alternate lifestyle, not abnormal behavior.

From previous experience, we knew that tangling with educators is like grabbing a tiger by the tail! The health teachers bristled when we suggested that some moral guidelines ought to be included in the course. *Not* teaching moral absolutes is a humanist view, and the Supreme Court has granted Secular Humanism tax-exempt religious status.

"I would not impose my religious views on children!" the

39

young female teacher exclaimed. "That is up to the parents and the church."

"Yes, but how do we know *when* to reinforce our religious principles when we didn't even know you were teaching sex education?" asked one parent.

"We have to teach about contraceptives because of the increase in venereal disease and premarital sex," the coach insisted. "But we can't teach morals."

Jim frowned quizzically. "You are a baseball coach, aren't you? Don't you teach right and wrong there? If your outfielder misses a cut-off man, don't you tell that player he's wrong?"

"Oh, we are concerned with moral values," one administrator interjected. He passed around a booklet used as a teacher guideline, *The Teaching of Moral and Spiritual Values.* Its Statement of Purpose was clear: "Many individuals and organizations across America are calling for an increased emphasis upon values clarification." It was mostly educational gobbledegook under a misleading cover title. There was no mention of moral absolutes—God's or anyone else's—and no suggestion of right or wrong. But certain code words and reference sources were the key to the booklet's intent.

"If fairness is to flourish in inter-relationships between teacher and students there must be consistency and some uniformity in all decisions and standards. Fairness is founded upon *equality,* so much as is *humanly* possible. Such *equality* lends a feeling of security, a sense of *'all-rightness'* to the situation. With this emerging sense of security there comes a developing of *tolerance* whereby those involved are willing to endure *allowable deviation* occasionally in order to keep the *situation* running smoothly. *Tolerance* is not a natural instinct, but must be encouraged and nurtured, *experience* by *experience."* (Emphasis added.)

It was a haunting rehash of John Dewey, the *Humanist Manifesto,* and the "equality" cry of Women's Lib. Tucked into the back cover pocket was a memorandum to teachers explaining that Federal Education Title II funds were used to purchase library materials on this subject. Listed were two NEA books, a set of filmstrips and cassettes comprised of "open-ended stories. . .in which a person is left with making a value judgment," and *Values Clarification,* by Sidney Simon, the prophet of this new teaching technique.

This was the author Dr. McGraw had been speaking about only two days earlier! Sidney Simon was *the* innovator of instructing children to redefine their values by accepting moral relativism, a sophisticated way of excusing immorality as defined by Biblical precepts.

While our parents' meeting did not succeed in convincing Junior High administrators to add so much as one class period for a pastor to bring the spiritual implications to bear on the subject, we did get the staff to separate easily embarrassed 12- and 13- year-old boys and girls during that unit. The previous year no parent had discovered that teaching of amoral sex education had quietly begun. And parents were surprised by the rumor that our small school system had a Junior High pregnancy that year!"

My interest in the extent of values clarification, however, was heightened and I began to check with teacher friends on its use in their schools. My research resulted in a column which I write as a member of the editorial board for a weekly newspaper.

VALUES CLARIFICATION—AN ATTACK ON PARENTS' RIGHTS

Scene: A fifth grade classroom of a public school
Enter: The district counselor
Counselor: Today I am going to help you clarify some of your personal values. Please raise your hand in answer to the questions I will ask. Feel free to question each other about why you answered as you did. *Question #1:* How many of you go to church regularly? *Question #2:* How many of you *like* to go to church? *Question #3:* If you could vote, would you vote the same as your parents?

Is this interaction merely an innocent game to get students to become better decision-makers, or is it a wedge driven between the values parents teach at home and the child who is encouraged at school to "choose" his own values?

41

While the term "values clarification" or "value judgments" sounds as if some kind of values are to be taught, quite the opposite is true. Instructors are cautioned that the child must not be made to feel that there is a right or wrong answer. The correct answer is whatever action or point of view the child *freely chooses* and practices. This methodology ignores the moral and religious values and standards practiced by the child's parents or church.

It is for these reasons that Alan L. Lockwood, University of Wisconsin education professor, wrote in "A Critical View of Values Clarification": "The moral point of view imbedded in values clarification is that of the ethical relativist. . .which holds that one person's values are as good as another's; everyone is entitled to his own opinion; and when it comes to morality, there is no way of showing one opinion is better than another. . .so it can be used to justify virtually any activity in which an individual or a society chooses to engage."

In another area school handbook on values clarification, we read: "Tolerance is not a natural instinct, but must be encouraged and nurtured. . ." Sounds fine—but, with no moral absolutes or norms allowed, as Lockwood points out, "assuming Adolph Hitler, Charles Manson, Martin Luther King and Albert Schweitzer held values that met the. . .criteria, are their values equally valid, praiseworthy, and/or good?"

Values clarification, like the Equal Rights Amendment, could well open a Pandora's box because "values" like "equal rights" is not defined! A lot depends, of course, on the teacher of values. If he or she is a practitioner of the Judeo-Christian faith, he can find this technique a useful tool in guiding students to choose the historic moral values, thereby reinforcing parental rights to childrearing. On the other hand, a secular humanist could use values clarification to discredit parental teaching and influence rebellion against all authority figures. Teacher's admonitions that "students should be encouraged to pursue the fulfillment of those values which are accepted by their society" could well be interpreted as peer-group values. . .not those of Western civilization.

Sex education is one example of subject matter that could create problems when grade school children are encouraged to make their own decisions without a standard of right or wrong on which to base these decisions. That is why Barbara Morris in her book *Why Are You Losing Your Children?* warns parents to be alert to the invasion of their child's privacy in the classroom: "In values clarification nothing is sacred. Everything your child values is up for grabs: religion, sex, family, friends, hair styles, death, war, authority. . . .Think of all the positive values you have tried to teach your children. . . . You didn't give them the option of 'choosing from alternatives'—why should you? In your maturity and judgment. . .you have taught them what you perceive to be right and proper."

Do you know if values clarification is being practiced on your child? Education *per se* is not infallible. Remember, some years ago educators threw out phonics—and produced a generation of children who could not read. Parents have rights, too—exercise them.

The parents of Kenawha County, West Virginia, did exercise their rights. They stirred up a hornets' nest by daring to stand against educational experts when their moral and religious values were ignored by textbooks inflicted on their children. God-fearing men and women were smeared by the media as religious fanatics, and the word "censorship" was bandied about in defense of the books.

But *Editor & Publisher* magazine admitted that there isn't any "newspaper in general circulation that is prepared to print the stuff verbatim." The objectional books contained profanities, obscenities, blasphemies, vulgarities, disrespect for parents, tolerance of violence, drinking and dope, and ungrammatical English.

In her January 1975 *Phyllis Schlafly Report,* my friend wrote: "It would be a mistake to consider the West Virginia textbook controversy a local matter. The same offensive textbooks are used in schools all over the country."

Indeed, they are. One of the literature books questioned in West Virginia is being used by our eighth grader in 1977! I wish I had caught the mother who left Craig's language arts room during Open House before I could reach her.

While the teacher was showing parents the text, she timidly

raised her hand. "I almost called the school when I read some of the stories in my daughter's book. They are so depressing and violent," she said.

Perhaps she was referring to the one about the cruel, senseless killing of a kitten.[2]

"Well, those stories are situations in real life," he replied brusquely. "We can't sugarcoat reality."

The gentleman is a fine teacher and a professing Christian. Unfortunately, like so many other educators, he has accepted on blind faith what the "experts" are promoting. Apparently, that one mother and I are the only two parents in our city of 15,000 who cared enough to take time to read our children's books. Had anyone suspected that a local cat-stomping incident, which left someone's pet dead, might have been prompted by the textbook?

"The hand that rocks the cradle, rules the world," is a self-evident truth. But with the siren song of Women's Lib, it may not be mother who rocks the cradle as frequently as education professionals. While even Christian mothers are being lured into full-time employment outside the home—distracting them from the nurture of their own children—three million dollars already has been allocated for a Federal White House Conference on Families (coordinating with the UN International Year of the Child in 1979) to design a new national policy for children.[3] It is a dear price to pay for LIBerty.

ERA Is *Not* a Laundry Detergent!

*"When the enemy shall come in like a flood,
the Lord will raise up a standard against him."—
Isaiah 59:19*

It already was after four o'clock in the afternoon, two hours
past the appointed time for the committee to hear testimony
on the Equal Rights Amendment. Sitting on a bench beside
the Speaker's rostrum with others scheduled to testify, I
noticed that the crush of demonstrators in the galleries was
beginning to thin. Most of the ERA YES signs were gone—
probably to catch the buses hired to bring proponents from
Chicago—and the majority of men, women and teenagers
were STOP ERA volunteers.

"The Lord is in control," I told myself, smiling.

Finally, the Speaker called the hearing to order. Practically
all the seats on the floor of the Illinois House were taken,

45

not only by members of the committee but by other representatives and senators interested in the proceedings. A few sipped coffee from paper cups, flipped aimlessly through newspapers, or talked in low tones to an aide.

The rules were set. Thirty minutes for each side. Questions by the committee would follow. The proponents went first. Attorneys, educators, union officials, officers of prominent organizations—even a Catholic nun who thought women ought to be priests—were given the utmost courtesy and warm applause.

Then Phyllis Schlafly, national chairman of STOP ERA, took the stand. Greeting a now-cool audience with a smile, she began explaining the pitfalls of doctrinaire equality.

Suddenly a female legislator broke in. "Mrs. Schlafly, we have agreed to disagree before. How can you expect us to believe that 'equality of rights under the law' can be harmful to women?"

The Speaker of the House rapped his gavel. "Please let the witness finish."

Phyllis smiled and continued, but before long a representative on the opposite side of House chamber interrupted. "Mrs. Schlafly, are you an attorney?"

"No, I am not. But I am quoting some of the most respected constitutional authorities including Professor Thomas Emerson of the Yale Law School who favors the amendment."

"Well, I am an attorney," he snapped, "and I know better."

The first of a long series of battles had begun. The Equal Rights Amendment had been introduced in every Congress since 1923. It had taken nearly fifty years of humanistic influence in education before ERA was finally approved by the U.S. House in 1971 and in the Senate on March 22, 1972. This proposed 27th Amendment to the U.S. Constitution reads:

Section 1: Equality of rights under the law shall not be denied or abridged by the United States or by any State on account of sex.

Section 2: The Congress shall have the power to enforce, by appropriate legislation, the provisions of this article.

Section 3: This amendment shall take effect two years after the date of ratification.

The Joint Resolution of the 92nd Congress required approval by three-fourths of the states within seven years. Hawaii was the first to ratify ERA within hours of the Senate's vote. Other states quickly followed suit. Feminists were jubilant. By 1975, 34 of the necessary 38 states had ratified.* Most of the uninformed public *thought* it meant equal pay for equal work for women.

Then the Lord intervened. He did not use a great statesman or famous writer or VIP. He chose a godly Christian woman in Miami, Florida. Shirley Spellerberg of WKAT had begun to research the legislative history of the Equal Rights Amendment, and convinced Phyllis Schlafly, mother of six, commentator on CBS' "Spectrum" and syndicated columnist for Copley News Service, of the inherent dangers. In February 1972, the *Phyllis Schlafly Report* carried the first alert to 5,000 subscribers—mostly Christians. The STOP ERA movement was launched!

We were certainly a little flock pitted against a formidable array of forces supporting the Women's Lib Amendment— the President, the Congress, the Federal bureaucracy, the mushrooming feminist organizations, the nationally respected League of Women Voters, Business and Professional Women and major religious denominations. Yet, we believed the Lord's admonition: "Know ye the truth, and the truth (not Women's Lib) shall make you free" (John 8:32). So we set out to tell the truth to American men and women and legislators in fifty states. Not even David facing Goliath could have been more overwhelmed!

Across the nation, Christian women took the message to Bible classes, Altar and Rosary societies, garden clubs, Republican and Democratic women, mother/daughter banquets,

---

*Ratified states: Alaska, California, Colorado, Connecticut, Delaware, Hawaii, Idaho (rescinded), Indiana, Iowa, Kansas, Kentucky (rescinded), Maine, Maryland, Massachusetts, Michigan, Minnesota, Montana, Nebraska (rescinded), New Hampshire, New Jersey, New Mexico, New York, North Dakota, Ohio, Oregon, Pennsylvania, Rhode Island, South Dakota, Tennessee (rescinded), Texas, Vermont, Washington, West Virginia, Wisconsin, Wyoming.

Wednesday night church meetings, Rotary, Kiwanis, college campuses, radio and television. Concerned citizens were asked to write their state legislators. Rallies were organized in our state capitols. We took loaves of homemade bread to "the bread-winners from America's bread bakers." In Illinois, we once baked nearly 400 apple pies for our lawmakers!

More than ten years before, I had promised the Lord that I would go anywhere to speak for Him. Little did I realize that after a decade of Bible study He would call me to be an ambassador for Him in the political arena.

In February 1974, a major evangelical family magazine printed an article I had written called "What's Behind the Equal Rights Amendment?" Thousands of requests flooded the publication's offices before they discontinued reprinting. Then in the summer of '75, I received a letter from a pastor in New York state. Both New York and New Jersey were gearing up for a referendum on a state ERA in November. Was I planning to publish an update that churches could use? Several months earlier, the Rev. Harry Middlebrooks of Tallahassee, Florida, had asked me to write a new article for a Methodist publication. It had been rejected because the denomination officially supports ERA.

My husband thought the minister's request was God's leading, so I copyrighted "A Christian View of ERA," and had a thousand copies printed. I had stepped out on faith. The day I placed the order with the Christian printer, I remarked, "I'm not sure how I'm going to pay the bill, but I'm trusting the Lord to provide!" When I opened the mail box that afternoon, there were two orders for the pamphlet. The combined checks were ten dollars short of the cost of typesetting and printing. The next day, a friend pressed a bill into my hand.

"Here's something to help you in your work," she said. It was ten dollars!

Two years after I first published "A Christian View of ERA," new evidence against the amendment had become important, so I wrote an "Update 1977." Finally, orders became so numerous that I gave permission for some states to print it locally. Since my first wobbly step of faith, I now order in lots of 5,000, and I have lost count of how many copies have been distributed in virtually every state. The total is perhaps in the hundreds of thousands.

I began the "Update" with a verse from Proverbs.

• • •

UPDATE 1977: A CHRISTIAN VIEW OF ERA

"There is a way which seemeth right unto man. . ." (14:12). And so it is with the Equal Rights Amendment in an increasingly secular world.

The New Testament makes it abundantly clear that all men and women are created equal in the sight of God. But as the Apostle Paul teaches, members of the body of Christ have various talents, abilities, roles—just as the human body has eyes, hands and feet—yet no member is less important than another. In the family, the husband is the provider; the wife is his helpmate and mother of his children—both equal but each with a special position. In society, as in Biblical history, women have a place in government, business, agriculture or even the military. . .as she is led by God, and as she and her husband agree.

Unfortunately, the far-reaching implications of the controversial Equal Rights Amendment will not take this Christian view into account.

"The ERA makes no exemptions or exclusions whatsoever for different treatment of the two sexes," writes the *St. Louis Globe-Democrat* editor. "Equality is absolute, total, unalterable for all time. What is good or bad for one sex is legally good or bad for the other, and lawmakers would be forbidden from ever distinguishing between the two on any matter. Therein lies the fatal flaw of ERA."

Proponents of the 27th Amendment to the U.S. Constitution speak in vague generalities about discrimination against women as a class, and how we are all eager to share equally in rights and responsibilities with men. Not surprisingly, they carefully neglect to define the drastic new responsibilities ERA would bestow on every woman. In fact, those advocating ERA—even in the religious community—never consider God's will for individual women.

49

Existing Equality Laws

To the average citizen, the Equal Rights Amendment simply implies equal pay for equal work regardless of sex. An examination of present Federal laws, however, shows that this right and many others already are guaranteed. The Equal Employment Opportunity Act of 1972 and the Civil Rights Act of 1964 require equal pay and job opportunity, leading to "affirmative action" programs with suggested quotas for men, women, ethnic minorities and blacks.

The Higher Education Act of 1972 prohibits sex discrimination in public education. Subsequently, the Title IX guidelines of the Department of HEW for enforcing equality in education are so comprehensive that all classes—elementary through college—must be coed. Not even all-boy or all-girl choirs are allowed. Exceptions are contact sports if there are alternative football, wrestling or boxing teams for women. (A 1978 Ohio court ruling mandates coed contact sports under the state ERA.) College fraternities and sororities still are permitted, and private or traditional single-sex schools are supposedly exempt. Even so, some universities receiving no Federal aid, such as Hillsdale College in Michigan or Brigham Young in Utah, are increasingly being pressured by HEW to drop their religious moral standards regarding separate dorms for men and women, making all housing sexually integrated. (These regulations would have made mother-daughter/father-son events illegal if President Ford had not interceded!)

In addition, the 1974 Housing and Community Development Act gives women equal credit. Of course, there are problems of unscrupulous persons who still practice discrimination. . . human nature being what God says it is. But by law, women are granted the equality they need without loss of those protections based on America's Judeo-Christian heritage.

Equal Responsibilities

Since "equal rights" already are a fact for women, what are the "equal responsibilities" that feminists supporting ERA say women must share with men? Because "equal rights" was not defined, the U.S. Congress attempted to clarify the meaning by proposing modifications to prevent unreasonable interpretation by the courts, thus preserving the values of Western culture. These amendments would have excluded women from combat in our present volunteer military and from the draft if it were ever revived; exempted working women from forced overtime and weightlifting; retained protections to wives, mothers or widows; imposed on fathers the primary responsibility for financial support of their children; and secured privacy to men and women.[1]

All these modifications to ERA, allowing reasonable distinction between men and women based on physiological or functional differences, were defeated! So when proponents try to soothe away apprehension over possible radical effects of ERA by saying the courts will abide by the "intent of Congress," we can be certain that the intent is, indeed, a dramatic restructuring of women's responsibilities. We can no longer assume that equality under the law will permit distinctions while forbidding discrimination.

As Dr. Francis Schaeffer said following the 1973 abortion decision, "The arbitrary absolutes of the Supreme Court are accepted against the previous consensus of centuries, as well as past law. . .We are left with sociological law without any certainty of limitation." A Court that disregards human life and takes away prayer in public schools will be free to interpret ERA any way it desires.

Certainly, the enthusiasts lobbying for equal responsibilities are not speaking for the majority of women.

Equality Vs. Biblical Truth

While Christians ought to be on the front lines in the battle against injustice, we are warned to "be not unequally yoked" and to beware of "wolves in sheep's clothing." Many sincere church bodies, theologians and clergy do not seem to understand that the Christian definition of equality is quite different from the equality envisioned by those most vocal in promoting ERA. Feminists glibly quote Galatians 3:28 that "there is no male or female. . .for all are one in Christ Jesus" while rejecting Scriptural principles. Instead, they seek a society where women are liberated from Christian truth.

51

As Betty Friedan, founder of NOW, asserts: "The second stage of the women's revolution is to restructure institutions. . .."

A prime mover in seeking passage of ERA, NOW's other priorities include:

Repeal of all abortion laws. In championing the "right to control her own body," feminists overlook the unborn's "right to life." In so doing, they deny mankind's creation in the image of God. Says Professor Joseph P. Witherspoon, University of Texas Law School: "Ratification of the ERA will inevitably be interpreted by the Supreme Court. . .as an approval by the people of the U.S. of its 1973 decision invalidating state anti-abortion statutes, and of its declaration therein that the unborn child is not a human person whose life is protected by the Constitution." Already under the edict, state laws requiring parents of teenagers and husbands to give consent to the abortion have been declared illegal!

Federal child-care. A task force—assisted by NOW—to implement Ohio's state ERA, determined that women encumbered with children are discriminated against because they are unable to be fulfilled by taking a job outside the home. This committee concluded that the state must establish child-care for all mothers regardless of economic need.[2]

Challenge of church tax-exempt status. Christians today may freely choose between congregations which do or do not ordain women, and assign different roles to men and women. But feminists insist that churches must conform to their idea of non-sexist equality or lose their tax-exempt status. . .a total perversion of the right to freedom of worship! Yet, Bob Jones University's tax status is in jeopardy because of the Supreme Court's strict civil rights opinion that clashes with BJU's religious beliefs.

Legalizing homosexual/lesbian marriages. Under Colorado's state ERA, two homosexuals were given a marriage license. Jack Baker, "gay" lawyer, says ERA will make marriage and adoption of children legal, and the *Yale Law Journal* supports this interpretation. While those outside the Judeo-Christian faiths may not object to these "different lifestyles," Holy Scripture forbids it.

This philosophy of feminism is expounded by Mary Daly in *Beyond God the Father: Toward a Philosophy of Women's Liberation:* "It is the women's movement which appears to play the key role in the overthrow of such oppressive elements in traditional theism. . . .It presents a growing threat to the plausibility of the inadequate popular 'God'. . . .Few major feminists display great interest in institutional religion."

Christian legislators, who have studied the amendment's ramifications and have debated proponents, can speak with some authority. Rep. Donna Carlson (Ariz.) says, "ERA is one of the most insidious schemes ever devised to destroy the very thing that has kept our country strong for 200 years—the home and the family." Delegate Eva Scott (Va.) believes, "ERA is unnecessary. It will hasten the erosion of the family. It will cause endless problems in schools and colleges by banning any difference of treatment between the sexes. And it will compel equal treatment for men and women in the military."

Federal Power Grab

Why are these and hundreds of other state legislators particularly concerned about the Federal government usurping power through ERA? Explains Sen. Joan Gubbins (Ind.): "As a state senator, sworn to uphold the Indiana and U.S. Constitutions, I must oppose further encroachment on individual citizens' rights and benefits. . . .Passage of ERA would subvert the Constitution by transferring many areas of law to the Federal level. It would make a mockery of the 10th Amendment under which rights concerning family and local affairs are 'reserved to the states respectively.'"

It is Section II of ERA which will transfer all power concerning women's rights and domestic relations out of the hands of the states and into the hands of an insensitive Federal bureaucracy. That is the reason four states have rescinded their hasty ratification. Unhappily, with the approval of Indiana in 1977 (made possible by Rosalynn Carter's promise to campaign for one senator if he would change his vote to "yes"), only three more states are needed to liberate our society from God's unique plan for men and women.

Foreshadowing of ERA

Advocates who publicly declare that no adverse effects have come to pass in states that have ratified ERA are like those depicted in Romans 1 who "professing themselves to be wise they became fools."

In the state of Washington, a protective labor law for women, restricting enforced overtime and weightlifting, has been abolished. Proponents falsely promise that new laws will not invalidate women's benefits but merely extend them to men under ERA. But it hasn't happened in Washington.

"It's not the old sweatshop," complains one female factory worker, "but the new modern sweatshop."[3]

Another storm of protest by parents was created in that state when separate dorms for men and women on college campuses were judged unconstitutional. Because ERA was not yet the law of the land, and only a state statute, the legislature was able to change this unreasonable policy.

Bear in mind, a U.S. Supreme Court ruling could not be altered if 38 states approve the 27th Amendment.

In Colorado, the state ERA is being implemented very slowly because of the problems experienced by other states which have attempted to make such changes. One controversial decision there overturned a law that made fathers responsible for the support of their children because the wife was not held equally liable.[4] What kind of equal rights is this for a mother of small children who may lack marketable skills?

Elsewhere, the Connecticut Supreme Court, subject to a state ERA, struck down the state's anti-abortion regulations *nine months before* the U.S. Supreme court's pronouncement.[5]

In the summer of 1976, U.S. Military Academies began accepting women who are now training to be combat officers. According to National Selective Service spokesman Brig. Gen. Sam Shaw, U.S.M.C.,[6] ERA would compel volunteer women to serve in combat. In any future conscription, no one knows how mothers and married women would be handled since they could not be classified by gender.

Never before in the history of Western civilization have women been forced into military conflict. While the Congress

54

always has had the power to draft women, it has chosen to exempt them. Not even in Israel, which does draft females because its very existence is at stake, do women serve in actual warfare. But ERA would leave Congress no choice. Although mothers of young children now enlist on a voluntary basis, Col. Nelda Cade, battalion commander, argues; "A woman's first duty is to her child and in the Army her first mission is the Army." Whereas ERA backers predict any future hostilities will be settled by negotiation, they willingly ignore Christ's warning that "there will be wars. . .until I come."

Although not a moral issue, Massachusetts' new state ERA is creating a hassle in the insurance industry because auto and life rates for females are lower based on statistics that show they have fewer accidents and live longer. Will women's insurance rates increase to become equal with men's? Clearly men's rates cannot be decreased without the insurer's financial loss.

And on the Federal level, how will Social Security be equalized? If homemakers are to be equal with employed persons, they must contribute to the system financially. The Fraser-Keys Bill (H.R. 3247) to amend the Social Security Act for such purposes was supported by the Illinois IWY meeting. That bill hopes to eliminate "dependent" status among married students.

As Sen. Prescott Bloom (Ill.) asks, "Has anyone done a cost-benefits analysis of ERA? I feel we all have a right to know what these benefits will be and their cost."

These are questions that will finally be answered by binding decisions of the Supreme Court, nine men appointed for life and not responsive to the voters, after ERA is ratified. Then it will be too late to do anything about it.

What Can Christians Do?

Today, the campaign to "liberate" us intensifies with biased pro-ERA media coverage, state-financed Status of Women Commissions, and the International Women's Year Commission with five million of your Federal tax dollars. As Christians, we should uphold enforcement of laws that provide equal opportunity for women, but we should oppose a sweeping change—a Constitutional "leap in the dark"—that could take away individual choices, and alter America's lifestyle. We must pray, but we must do more, for "faith without works is dead."

Immediate action—letters to *state* legislators asking them to rescind or to vote "no" on ERA—is urgent. Proponents claim states cannot rescind—that is change their vote from "yes" to "no"; but they insist a "no" vote can be changed to "yes." In fact, they are now asking Congress to extend the ERA ratification time for up to seven more years under the same unfair rules!

Jesus cautioned believers to beware of Satan coming as an angel of light so that even the elect will be deceived. We need to discern between spiritual equality before God and legal equality before Caesar. Let us be very careful that the "innocent" Equal Rights Amendment does not become another apple for Eve!

• • •

With no financial backing from *Playboy,* state or Federal resources, or foundations, STOP ERA—one of the greatest ecumenical movements in the history of America—has operated on a shoestring with proceeds from bake sales, small contributions, and money carefully budgeted from sugarbowl savings. Prayer chains have spread across entire states as mainline Protestants, fundamental independents, Roman Catholics, Mormons and Orthodox Jews work together to convince legislators that the majority does not want or need the Equal Rights Amendment.

We have founded loosely structured organizations by a dozen or more names: Women Who Want to be Women (WWWW's), Happiness of Womanhood (HOW), Women for Responsible Legislation, Operation Wake-Up, and Eagle Forum to name a few. Other established groups joined in opposing the amendment: Veterans of Foreign Wars, various state Farm Bureaus, several state Federated Women's Clubs, National Council of Catholic Women, Rabbinical Society of America, Southern Baptists, Missouri Synod Lutherans,

Churches of Christ, Daughters of the American Revolution, and the National Right to Life are included.

By October 1977, the Women's Lib Amendment had floundered—stalled three states short of ratification with only 18 months left to ratify. We stood to close the annual STOP ERA National Conference with Ann McGraw, a Christian School music teacher, leading us in singing the prayer, "God Bless America." I felt a lump in my throat and I noticed tears in many eyes as our unique fellowship of believers in Almighty God asked His blessing upon our land.

Women Are Persons

"A sufficient measure of civilization is the influence of good women."—Ralph Waldo Emerson

Since 1972, when the battle over the Equal Rights Amendment began, the local founder of NOW and I had been debating before women's and civic clubs. This time we were speaking to the combined social studies classes of a large city high school.

As the Illinois director of Eagle Forum—"the alternative to Women's Lib"—I had been forewarned that one of the team-teachers was not sympathetic to our traditional views of God, home and country. As the discussion progressed, however, he kept a low profile as a neutral moderator.

The NOW representative presented the typical feminist line. Although she was married, she said she would not take her husband's surname because, unless she retained her maiden name, she would not be a person in her own right. The boys in the class were miffed.

"I would want my wife to take my last name," one young man protested.

"What will you do about your children's name?" another inquired. "Will they use your name or your husband's?"

"Well, we really haven't decided if we even want children," she replied. "They might choose to take a hyphenated name of both of ours."

"Whose name will you put first?" smirked a third youth.

In a stage whisper, another teen observed, "She is still using a man's name—her father's!"

Her response to other questions parroted feminists across the nation and around the world. She saw no problem with women in combat. After all, didn't mothers love their sons as much as their daughters? And who would worry about personal privacy in the trenches anyway, because today's women want to share rights and responsibilities equally! Insisting that women have the "right to control their own bodies," she claimed that a Pro-Life Amendment to the Constitution would impose certain religious beliefs on everyone—not guarantee an unborn child's right to live. And, of course, she pointed out that as long as churches have tax-exempt status, they should not be able to discriminate against women, minorities or homosexuals by refusing to ordain them as pastors and priests. (NOW is on record as supporting lesbian rights and restructuring churches.)

"Most women want to take their husband's name at marriage whether they choose to be full-time homemakers or pursue a career," I replied. "Being Mrs. James Thomson does not take away my 'personhood.' I am known and respected in the community for my own volunteer activities, like helping pass a school bond referendum and as a free-lance writer for Christian publications."

Regarding abortion, I contrasted humanist beliefs with Biblical truths. "Therefore, abortion is—in the secular sense— a violation of the 14th Amendment which prohibits depriving 'any person of life.' "

And finally, I defined Eagle Forum's position of the right of all religious bodies to designate different roles among their members for men and women without government interference. (I was careful not to promote any specific religion while explaining different convictions.)

The class was nearly over when the teacher raised his hand. "I would like you both to comment on a verse from Genesis," he said opening a Bible. "To the woman God said, I will greatly multiply your pain in childbearing; in pain you shall bring forth children, yet your desire shall be for your husband, and he shall rule over you."

I was dumbfounded. He was the last person I would have expected to give an opportunity in a public classroom to openly share the meaning of God's Word.

"Dear Lord," I prayed silently, "give me the right thing to say."

My opponent bristled. "I refuse to comment. Religion has no bearing on ERA!"

Since feminists usually avoid exposing their true religious beliefs publicly, I knew why she was unwilling. Several years before, she had told me privately that she had formerly been a Catholic, had converted to Judaism during her first marriage, and now practiced no faith.

"That is quite a theological question," I said, drawing a long breath. In that split second, my mind flashed back to the research I had been helping our 7th grade son dig out for a science report on creation vs. evolution. I would base my answer on the obvious design of nature. . .chaos vs. order.

"Perhaps I can simplify it this way," I said. "Christians believe that God has a plan for the universe. He designed our world to operate in an orderly sequence. The earth turns on its axis, bringing the seasons. The stars, sun and moon stay in their orbits. All we need do is look at nature to see that everything happens on schedule. God is the authority who created this plan.

"In business and government, too, there is always someone in authority who must make the final decision. And so in God's plan for families, someone must be the chairman. He created men and women equal in His sight, but He assigned different, distinct roles to the husband and wife. Both are persons in their own right, but as in any organization, someone must be chief executive. In God's orderly arrangement for harmonious family living, he appointed the husband president."

There was silence for a moment. Then one blue-jeans-clad girl who had been arguing for feminism all period exclaimed, "I don't want to talk about religion. This discussion is offensive to me!"

The bell rang. Class was over.

As the female counterpart of the teaching team walked me to the door, she confided her resentment of Women's Lib. "My son married a feminist. At first he thought it was cute. The day after their wedding, she went down to the Court House to change her name back to her maiden name. Then she insisted on separate bank accounts. She didn't want to share anything with my son. It ended up not to be a joke." She sighed. "That girl totally emasculated him. They are divorced now."

Why are modern feminists clamoring that women are not persons? Can a Christian woman be submissive to her husband as the Bible commands, and still keep her identity as a unique personality important to God? Or as an Illinois legislator—an attractive grandmother whom I have debated—insists, are we still considered chattel by archaic laws? This pressure to "be someone" accosts women daily.

Even missionary Lucille Cole succumbed to this temptation. As a tape editor for HCJB radio—broadcasting around the world from high in the Andes at Quito, Equador—she began to feel irritation toward her husband. Lou told me how the Lord helped her resolve this conflict, following a talk I gave on "Freedom in Femininity" at the Wheaton (Ill.) Evangelical Free Church.

"Nothing in Dick's background prepared him for a wife who had creative interests outside the home," Lou recalled. "My hunger for involvement in music, dramatics and writing was puzzling, even threatening to him. He was a loving, faithful husband, providing fully for our demanding family. Why couldn't I be satisfied? In my frustration I wavered between guilty martyrdom and resentment, unable to pinpoint the cause of my spiritual dissatisfaction. If God is the source of abundant life, then surely I couldn't blame Dick for my lack.

"I'm glad God is patient. It took me several years to discover that the difference between meekness and martyrdom, between femininity and feminism is a matter of priority! The Lord showed me that martyrdom says, 'I will squelch my desires and do something I hate.' Meekness says, 'I want to do God's will.' Feminism insists, 'I have the right to do what I wish.' Femininity asks, 'How can I help you?' Personal need isn't ignored or suppressed. It is simply put in a lower order of priority."

As Lou talked, I recalled what Jesus once said: "Whosoever will be chief among you, let him be your minister, and whosoever will be chief among you, let him be your servant; even as the Son of man came not to be ministered unto, but to minister, and to give his life a ransom for many" (Matthew 20: 26-28). This missionary wife was putting into the vernacular Paul's teaching, "Let this mind be in you, which was also in Christ Jesus" (Philippians 2:5). And I was reminded of Luke 12:31—the key to opening my own understanding: "Seek ye first the kingdom of God, and all these things shall be added unto you."

Then Lou described the fantastic results of her spiritual discovery. "As my husband saw me wholeheartedly putting my family before myself, he hesitantly began to suggest outside activities for me. It was as though with each new endeavor he would check to see if the family really came first. Then Dick actually urged me to start working for my master's degree in broadcast communications. The classes were stretching and exciting, but about halfway through they began disrupting the household and putting added responsibility on him at home—just at a time when his work was particularly discouraging.

"One evening as we lingered over after-dinner coffee, breakfast dishes—a job that had fallen to him—still stacked in the sink, I asked Dick truthfully, 'Honey, do you want me to quit? You know you and the kids mean more to me than a degree.'

"After a long pause, in which he considered the honesty of his reply, he answered, 'Not really. I'm just tired. I'd be disappointed if you gave up now.'

"There had been a time—before I had allowed Christ to liberate me from myself—when my question would have been an accusation; his response a resounding 'Yes!' But now, proper priority has led me to fulfillment in a living liberty under God that truly is abundant life."

Here is the solution to real "personhood" for a Christian woman—not from manmade laws or feminists' "strikes for equality"—but from aligning her will with the perfect will of God! Lucille Cole is one of hundreds of women who have become "persons in their own right" because they followed God's formula for success.

Senator Joan Gubbins is an example of how Christ often liberates women to positions of leadership when they seek and act upon Biblical principles. Mrs. Gubbins, a contented housewife, began to read her children's textbooks, and became concerned as she saw Christian values deleted from literature and social studies books. She began working in political campaigns, hoping to turn Indiana schools "back to basics" by electing candidates who opposed humanistic education.

"I had never made a speech before in my life," Senator Gubbins told me in an interview on Channel 13-TV, Peoria. "But I found myself quite unexpectedly nominated for state senator by a Republican caucus because no one else wanted to run! I learned very quickly to make public speeches, encouraged by my husband, Dale, as I sought God's will for the election. I believe He must have given me the 'gift of governments,' since I am now in my third term in the Senate."

Shirley Curry, minister's wife, mother and college professor, believed God's plan for wives submitting to their husbands. Result: the rescinding of the Equal Rights Amendment by the state of Tennessee!

As a working woman, Mrs. Curry favored ERA. . .until a friend gave her a copy of testimony before the Senate Judiciary Committee in *The Congressional Record.*

"I was complaining to my husband about the terrible effects of ERA, wringing my hands and fussing that someone should do something!" she told me. "Jess looked up from the sermon he was preparing. 'Shirley,' he suggested, 'why don't you do something? Perhaps, like Queen Esther, you have been called to the kingdom for such a time as this.'"

She took his advice, drove to the state Capitol and told her senator she wanted to have Tennessee rescind ERA. It was a noble goal, he said, and although Nebraska recently had been the first state to do so, he guessed it would take several years to accomplish.

With the help of Tottie Ellis, another Church of Christ pastor's wife, Shirley mobilized Christian women throughout the state.

"When we descended on the Capitol, the legislators thought there were thousands of us," Shirley says. "We wore STOP ERA buttons and lined up along the hallways and in front of the chamber doors to the House and Senate. Everywhere they went, there we were!"

It took only six weeks of work and prayer before the Tennessee legislature voted to reject the Equal Rights Amendment!

Are submissive wives really second-class citizens? If women can achieve in education, be elected to public office, and dramatically influence legislation, how can feminists claim "the U.S. Constitution doesn't consider women as persons"? Even under secular law, the Supreme Court increasingly uses the 14th Amendment to repeal laws which unfairly discriminate against women. The most striking application was a unanimous decision in Reed v. Reed, November 1971. It found the Idaho statute which gave preference to fathers over mothers in administering the estate of a deceased child violated the equal protection clause, since it provided "dissimilar treatment for men and women" who were "similarly situated."

Other inequalities can be corrected by specific legislation too. Unfair estate taxes paid by widows on family farms for example, were corrected by the 1976 Federal Tax Reform Act.

Dorothy Frooks, former suffragette, explodes the feminist myth that women are second-class citizens. "At present, by law, women have every right. To vote, to seek office, equal job opportunities. I know," says attorney Frooks. "I fought for all of them. But the ERA is a dangerous move. It will destroy the home and thus destroy the nation."

Granted, getting our priorities in order does not always come easily. But as Shirley Curry, Eagle Forum national board member, suggested in one newsletter: "Set goals! Short-term and long-term goals are necessary if we are to win success. How can we know we have attained our goal unless we first know what we intended to do? The battle for high morals and godly patterns always will remain unfinished business. Like the striving for perfection, there is no place to quit. Once a warrior enters the troop, it is a lifetime commitment."

Shirley's application for Christian women's role in society concludes: "Let us put on the full armor and go forth to attain our objective of keeping America great by keeping America good!"

Is Employment a Right for Everyone

"Many are destined to reason wrongly; others not to reason at all; and others to persecute those who do reason."—Voltaire

Jean's Beauty Shop was buzzing with comments pro and con. For several weeks as we sat under the hairdryers we had been reading Marabel Morgan's book, *The Total Woman*, which our Christian beautician had left on the coffee table.

"It's just great," one young mother insisted. "And I'd like to take the Total Woman Seminar!"

"I'm afraid Marabel Morgan has fallen into a feminist trap," I disagreed. "ERA proponents will use the book to 'prove' that all of us opposing the 27th Amendment are mindless slaves to chauvinist husbands."

"Here comes Elaine," Jean said, spraying my comb-out. "Ask her how she handles a job and homemaking."

The mother of two, Elaine Sutter is a dedicated second grade teacher. "That's easy," she said, smiling. "My direction is from the Lord, but it's not the exact way for every woman. Marriage to me is based on the Biblical principle of honoring and loving your husband. You know, Ephesians 5—he is the head of the house and all that. So my life plans are in accordance with Les' cooperation. That way I am free and happy in fulfilling what I feel called to do.

"That sounds awfully idealistic, doesn't it?" she continued. "But it's true. And Les is very interested in my educational accomplishments and professional opportunities."

"He doesn't feel threatened by them?" the young mother ventured.

"Oh no, he was the one who encouraged me to get my degree so I could teach!" Elaine answered.

The Sutters had married after graduation from Moody Bible Institute and were parents of a daughter before Elaine went back to the local university to complete requirements for her B.A. and master's degree.

"It was the best thing that happened to my family. Over the next several years the three of us shared cultural events on campus—like a performance by an Austrian cellist, a Roger Williams piano concert, and a showing of Grandma Moses' paintings," she recalled. "These experiences were enriching to us as a family, and helpful to our daughter in her school activities, too. And when I started teaching, we continued to enjoy interesting things together."

Their way of life was dramatically changed when, at 39, Elaine again became pregnant. Did she consider abortion?

"I have always prayed for the Lord's leading, and I knew that if I ever had to leave the educational field, He would help me do it," she explained. "We were all thrilled with our unexpected blessing, even though we knew each of our lives would face various adjustments."

Even after fifteen and one-half years without a baby, God guided Elaine in getting accustomed to her role as a new mother to a second sweet baby girl. She stayed home for eight months, and then as another school year rolled around she became eager to teach.

"I guess it's difficult to explain how much I love my family and how much I love teaching those precious little ones," she said. "But it's true that God gives you the desires of your heart, and He worked out a way for me to have the privilege of both motherhood and a career. Still, I advocate the principle of a mother's being in the home with her children. The key is God's leading and a husband's support."

But Women's Lib considers neither God's will nor a husband's feelings. As one feminist shouted at the National Women's Conference during the debate on employment, "It is the right of every able-bodied woman to have a job!"

Although proponents insist that ERA would give women a choice of working or being a full-time homemaker, Pro-Family women fear that gender-free equality would have exactly the opposite effect. Moreover, recent actions by courts and by industry to comply with the Equal Pay Act and Federal Affirmative Action Guidelines foreshadow the consequences of ERA on working women and heads of households.

Until some states added ERA to their constitutions, all laws required that the husband was responsible for the financial support of his wife in an ongoing marriage, and that he was liable for support of his children upon divorce. The distinguished constitutional lawyer, Professor Paul A. Freund of Harvard Law School opposes the amendment because one of the effects would be that wives and mothers would lose their legal right to be supported by their husbands. Professor Freund points out that the U.S. Citizens' Advisory Council on the Status of Women came up with the interpretation that "a husband should be liable only for the support of a wife who is unable to support herself due to a physical handicap, acute state of family responsibility or unemployability on other grounds."[1] The implication is that if child care centers are available, a wife with small children would no longer be exempt from taking a job because of family responsibility!

"What will be the reaction of wives to the Equal Rights Amendment," asks the professor, "when husbands procure judicial decisions in its name relieving them of the duty of support because an equal duty is not imposed on their wives?"

Prior to one ERA hearing in the Illinois Senate, a proponent asked me, "Don't you feel guilty that you don't work and your poor husband has all the responsibility to support you?"

This is exactly what feminists mean when they glowingly talk about equal rights and responsibilities. ERA could have a similar effect on Social Security benefits for wives who have not worked outside the home. For those of us who are full-time homemakers, present law provides retirement benefits under our husband's Social Security account. Financial columnist Sylvia Porter suggests that ERA would require homemakers to pay F.I.C.A. taxes, too!

"Of course, those taxes would have to come out of the earnings of the husband," Ms. Porter explains, "and it might be charged that he would be paying taxes twice—once on his own earnings and once on the assumed earnings of his wife—but this would be fair and equitable."[2]

For some families, the additional taxes may put such a strain on their budget that a wife would be forced to seek paid employment. In fact, Ms. Porter sees more working wives as a way to solve long-range problems of financing the struggling Social Security system: "More productive work and, therefore, more Social Security taxes will be paid by women who will be in paying jobs because they have fewer children," she explains.

Secretary of Commerce Juanita Kreps notes that "what both sexes might reasonably demand is shorter work weeks— or work interspersed with longer vacations, sabbaticals, education and training. This pattern would be especially helpful if men and women come to share more evenly the home work as they are now sharing the market work."

A 1975 ruling of Iowa's Merit Employment Commission shows how equal rights already have backfired on senior women. Two ladies, 62 and 64, are now required to unload 30-to 50-pound cases from trucks as well as to perform as sales clerks because of the "equal pay for equal work" concept.

"That's happening right here in Illinois!" a middle-aged widow told me. "I had worked my way up from checker in a supermarket chain to second office girl. Now all employees are forced to do equal work and receive equal pay whether we like it or not. I'm having to get up at 4 a.m. even on cold, snowy mornings to unload trucks. I've been told that if I don't do it, I'll be fired. I have to support my family so I don't dare object—I'd rather have a little less salary and not have to do the heavy lifting."

Naomi McDaniel, national president of Women of Industry, speaks for women who work on assembly lines: "The uninformed but noisy minority of ERA proponents—smooth talking college women who have never seen a factory production line—claim that some women can lift up to 75 pounds and should have the 'opportunity' to work alongside men. We Women of Industry know better than anyone else that we are simply not physically equal to men, but ERA permits no distinctions."[3]

"Equality" in employment can mean restructuring of attitudes as well. Consider firefighters and police officers. ERA would mandate identical treatment for men and women in these crucial public services. Equal assignments for women who may be physically unable to carry a heavy person from a burning building or subdue a criminal might jeopardize a life-or-death situation. In Chicago and Detroit, when women could not pass the same physical tests as men, they went into court to get the tests thrown out.

Another aspect is discussed by a New York Police Department psychologist: "In a car, partners share what we call 'intimate space.' This evolves into an 'us against them' relationship, which becomes a deep emotional relationship. Sexual tension has to be there between a man and a woman under those circumstances."

"That is why I filed suit on behalf of we truckers' wives," Oklahoma Pro-Family delegate Maxine Hamon told me at the National Women's Conference. "No way do we want our husbands paired with a female driver on cross-country hauls!"

In San Diego, firemen's wives object to lady firefighters sharing the same sleeping quarters with the firemen. Complained one angry wife, "With that kind of setup, you no longer will find the firemen whiling away the time between fire alarms over a game of checkers."

A 1977 study by the Law Enforcement Assistance Administration concluded that police women showed less physical strength and agility than men. Women also took sick leave more often, but the report could not determine if women were sick more often or if they stayed home to care for ailing family members. Pregnant police officers can create knotty discrimination problems, too. In Chicago, when an expectant patrol officer asked to be reassigned to a desk job, officials were in a quandary. Would men cry "foul" since they could never qualify for special treatment? Application of the theory of equal rights is not always practical.

There are other circumstances where reasonable discrimination would (and should) benefit women. A panel of experts on occupational health at the 1975 American Association for the Advancement of Science meeting agreed that women workers may face perils from dangerous chemicals. Since 60 percent of pregnant women stay on the job during their first pregnancy, risks to the fetus constitute the greatest danger.[4] Sex differences rarely are considered in studies of work hazards at present, but they would be forbidden under ERA. Yet the American Association for the Advancement of Science joined NOW's vindictive convention boycott of unratified states in 1978!

While feminists are pushing more and more women into the labor market, they seem oblivious to the unemployment problem. Nearly half of all wives are employed today, as well as half of all mothers with children under 18, according to the U.S. Labor Department. That makes 28.2 million children with working mothers, an increase of 10 percent in six years. The IWY National Plan of Action's summary background on employment despaired that men earn more than women and that the gap keeps widening.

"If you think about it," Elaine Donnelly, Michigan STOP ERA chairman, told us at a speaker's seminar, "the earnings gap will continue to widen. Women who are now going back to work have lost seniority by taking time out to have children. There is no way they can ever catch up with men who have continued to work during those years, but it has nothing to do with discrimination."

So when comparing the salary of a male electrical engineer who has worked 15 years and a female electrical engineer who has worked only 5 years, there naturally will be a wage gap.

That is why University of Illinois professor Marianne Ferber cautions wives about the "consequences of accepting the traditional role of the homemaker, because women who quit their jobs to raise a family and do not return to work may eventually regret their decision." Co-author of a new economic model for families, she continues, "If there were a rational division of tasks, husbands would take on a greater share of housework when a wife gets a job."

Senator Charles H. Percy echoed these anti-family sentiments at the Illinois IWY Women's meeting.

"The women's movement will not be successful if women alone pursue it and men are spectators. We must pursue it together. Remember, before men can be free, women must be free," he told us. "The threat to men is perceived as largely economic; for women the threat is more complex and personal. But changing human roles will mean all individuals will be able to live up to their full potential. . . . The time is long overdue for the molds to be thrown away—for men and women. And a society that stifles the potential of more than half its population is more than prejudiced and discriminatory. It is foolish and wasteful as well."

Wasteful—because all women do not have a paycheck from which income taxes are paid to finance government child development programs? Some women work because they are heads of households, others because God has led them to a profession. But where will the additional jobs come from if all mothers go to work?

"One reason for the high unemployment rate is that more and more people, particularly married women, are now seeking work who had never previously done so. Forty-five percent of married women now are working, compared with 30 percent just eleven years ago," explains Congressman Robert H. Michel, U.S. House Minority Whip (R.-Ill.). "If the 30 percent rate still prevailed today, there would be seven million more jobs available."

However, in 1975, Betty Friedan told an International Women's Day rally in New York that economic adversity was no reason for women to give up gains they have made in employment. "Women giving up their jobs to make way for male breadwinners won't solve the economic problems."[5]

Is employment a right for everyone? For Christian women, that answer is between them and the Lord.

G.I. Jill

"The inescapable price of liberty is an ability to preserve it from destruction."—Douglas MacArthur

"Karen has what?" I exclaimed in disbelief.

Lorie giggled. "Joined the Army!" she repeated. "I certainly never raised my daughter for that! Actually, it's the Army Reserve. Karen will have to go for two weeks basic training, then she'll have duty weekends."

When Karen first saw the Army's advertisement, she thought, "What a joke. They'll never take a married woman with a 15-month-old daughter."

Not only did the Army induct her, but she was placed in a combat artillery unit.

During the 1974 truckers' strike, a husband and his six-month pregnant wife, both members of the Illinois National

74

Guard, were called into active duty. They had a three-year-old child at home. The same year, the Navy hospital ship *Sanctuary* took on female crew members.

These examples point up how disruptive to family life the drafting of women would be. Yet Illinois legislator John Edward Porter, who intends to vote for the 27th Amendment, says, "ERA would make it constitutionally impossible to assign all females to non-combat jobs. . . .I do not think they should be exempted from these roles solely on the basis of sex."

These hard facts are glossed over by promoters of an ERA unisex society. The National Plan of Action, which each National Women's Conference delegate received, sidesteps these issues of the draft and evades the true impact. It states:

"It is fair to say that adoption of ERA *will:*
Insure equal opportunity, privileges and benefits in *all* aspects of government employment, including voluntary admission to the military services and military training schools...

"The ERA *will not:*
Alter family structure;
Require that there be *as many* women as men in combat roles. . ."

Distinguished military journalist Hanson W. Baldwin does not sugar-coat reality: "It is my belief that this change is destructive—not constructive—to the military and to our past way of life. If it is fortified and perpetuated by the passage of the Equal Rights Amendment, the internal problems the services face. . .will be tremendously magnified, and the nation's family structure—the basis of any stable society—will inevitably be weakened.

"The fundamental purpose [of military academies] is to produce the hard core of the nation's trained and dedicated fighting men. . ." explains Baldwin, himself a graduate of the U.S. Naval Academy. "The service schools exist to produce professional combat officers. . . .Physical aptitude tests for admission to the service academies already have been altered to meet one physiological difference between male and female in arm, chest and shoulder muscles. If the ERA is ratified, or the law prohibiting women in combat ships and planes is repealed, I believe the military effectiveness of the armed services, even now too low, will be seriously degraded.

"The family. . .has been the basic building block of stability. Yet, if the traditional male role of the father, as principal bread winner, protector and fighter, is smudged or obliterated; if the female tends to fill this role, family stability, already imperiled in too many American homes, will be further eroded. Women in combat and passage of ERA probably would represent an additional step towards family disintegration."[1]

Whose word should we believe? That of a military authority or the International Women's Year Commission? Alan Alda, TV star of M*A*S*H*, was an original member of the IWY. Imported to Illinois to testify before the General Assembly in favor of ERA, Alda—when asked if his three daughters would be conscientious objectors—replied, "I hope so."

Although the military academies and the Federal government keep publicly reporting that the women enrolled are "doing super," General William Westmoreland predicted the bona-fide consequences the spring prior to induction of the first females to the Long Gray Line.

"Maybe you could find one woman in 10,000 to lead in combat," he said, "but she would be a freak, and we're not running the Military Academy for freaks. . .I don't believe women can carry a pack, live in a foxhole, or go a week without taking a bath."

Three months after enrolling, one of the female cadets leaving West Point admitted, "Over the summer I became more frustrated with the running and foot marches. Even in marching, with my short legs I had trouble keeping up, striding the same length as the persons next to me, and I also ended up at the end of my platoon in the very last rank."

Furthermore, the former cadet couldn't visualize herself in combat, but she felt that the three months wasn't wasted because she had learned a lot.

But American taxpayers are not in the business of providing free education at military academies to females who do not intend to defend our country. Where does the "right" of a feminist to free education fit in with the "right" of all Americans to be protected in a desperate situation?

Notwithstanding that all military non-combat jobs now are open to women, the U.S. General Accounting Office reports that many positions are not being handled effectively by women because of their physical limitations. Some cannot lift 100-pound sandbags, 94-pound paint cans and boat lines that weigh up to 7 pounds a foot.

"As a result, men must perform a disproportionate share of the work," says GAO.

And what happens to a well-trained female pilot who gets pregnant? Lt. Barbara Rainey, the Navy's first woman pilot resigned! Mrs. Rainey, wife of a Navy pilot, could have taken maternity leave and returned to duty. Whatever Lt. Rainey's reason, how many mothers want to be out on a search-and-destroy mission when her baby is home in its bassinet?

Lest there be any doubt that the military intends to maintain expectant mothers in service, in November 1977, the Navy announced the designs of maternity uniforms for pregnant officers and enlisted women!

Civilian attorney Brenda Feign Fasteau, a feminist, appeared on "Good Morning, America" recently, promoting women in combat. But some women in the Marine Corps object.

Says Cherie St. Clair, 18, of Milford, Michigan, "I wouldn't have signed up if I thought I'd have to fight. And if ERA gets passed, I'll get out of the Marines as soon as I can."

Lt. Col. Vera Jones, commanding officer of the Women's Training Command at Parris Island, South Carolina, said she might give up her 16-year military career rather than face combat.

"I served in Vietnam as a personnel officer, and that was close enough [to combat] for me," Jones insists. "The idea of going to the lines is one thing that would send me running out to find a new job."

These are the reasons that the 76th National Convention of the Veterans of Foreign Wars of the U.S. passed a resolution against the Equal Rights Amendment.

Still, feminists have many slick answers which obscure facts.

Anne Follis, an attractive young minister's wife, is frequently my opponent in debates.

"Under ERA women will be able to volunteer for military service on the same basis as men and will receive the same benefits," Anne says. "If the draft is reinstated, women will be subject to it—and exempted from it—on the same basis as men. Mothers of young children undoubtedly would be exempted as fathers have been in the past."

"Women *already* can volunteer for military service on the same basis as men with the exception of combat units," I respond. "Girls are required to have a high school education. But do we want our first line of defense to be female high school dropouts? And how will mothers be exempted if laws must become sex-neutral? No one knows how the courts will interpret equality!"

The National Federation of Business and Professional Women (BPW) hedges on that question: "Congress will retain ample power to create legitimate sex-neutral exemptions. . . they might be extended to all parents of children under 18. . ."[2]

That fills the foxholes with aging parents of grown children! But, as BPW vacillates, "Women will share in the opportunity to defend their country. America deserves the best from all its citizens."

The League of Women Voters consoles women with the statistic that only one percent of eligible men are ever assigned to combat units. However, translated to real people, how many hundreds of POWs suffered at the hands of Viet Cong torturers; how many thousands died in the jungles of Southeast Asia in an undeclared war?

Another way feminists duck these "scare tactics" is to point out that there is no draft, so the question is moot. They imply that with IWY "peace" objectives, war will become obsolete. In place of church services on Sunday morning during the National Women's Conference, a Peace Hearing was conducted by Congresswoman Patricia Schroeder (D.-Colo.). Its thrust was general and complete disarmament.

A hand-out bearing the IWY official peace dove insignia stated, "Peace is a woman's issue. . . .We must urge that the United States demand the implementation of the 1961 Agreement on Goals at the Special Session on Disarmament at the United Nations General Assembly, May 1978."

These disarmament plans, agreed upon by the U.S. and the Soviet Union on September 20, 1961, and accepted by all UN members, supposedly would ensure total disarmament, peaceful settlement of disputes, and a maintained international peace. They would allow all member nations *only* sufficient non-nuclear armaments and forces to provide internal police protection for security of citizens. Each country would then furnish financial and manpower support for a United Nations Peace Force.

Inscribed on the "Isaiah Wall" at the United Nations in New York is a portion of Isaiah 2:4, ". . .and they shall beat their swords into plowshares, and their spears into pruning hooks; nation shall not lift up sword against nation, neither shall they learn war anymore." The most important part of the verse is omitted: "And He [Christ] shall judge among the nations."

Humanism in its most extreme form has announced to the world that man—not God—will bring peace. It rejects the context of Old Testament prophecy—the second coming of Jesus Christ, the Christians' only hope of world peace. In His place, the United Nations offers a "Peace Force."

If the UN is, indeed, the "last best hope of peace," as many claim, then it offers precious little hope. Since its founding in 1945, a police action, civil uprising or undeclared war has been in progress somewhere on the face of the globe. As much as we dream of world peace it is foolish to cry, "Peace, peace when there is no peace" (Jeremiah 8:11). From every quarter, both here and abroad, come warnings that Russia is arming for a first-strike capability. The U.S.S.R. has broken SALT treaty[3] agreements, and there is no disputing that their bloated tank artillery and ground personnel could sweep across Western Europe with little resistance!

Nevertheless, the Peace and Disarmament Resolution actually passed by the National Women's Conference reads: "The President and the Congress should intensify efforts to build, . . .an international framework within which serious disarmament negotiations can occur; reduce military spending. . . support peace education in schools. . ."

79

It is as though our country has not been engaged in years of signing arms limitation treaties with Russia, only to have them broken when the Soviets see fit to do so! The key to the so-called peace initiative lies in the second part of the UN agreement. All countries will retain "only such non-nuclear armaments, forces, facilities and establishments as are agreed to be necessary to maintain internal order." To put it another way, the United States would have no protection from an outside aggressor. Only the United Nations Peace Force would have arms.

Has IWY noticed that the U.S. is consistently outvoted in UN decisions? And is this a "women's rights" issue?

Pro-Family delegate Violet Hamilton made an important observation at the NWC Peace Hearing: "IWY commissioner Ethel Taylor was a member of the panel. Ms. Taylor is the national coordinator of 'Women Strike for Peace,' a feminist disarmament group which Bella Abzug helped organize."

Does IWY's "peace" smack of chairperson Abzug's "fight for peace" to prevent aid for the "imperialist aims of Britain" during the early years of World War II?[4] What will happen if women with this type of reasoning are appointed to positions in the executive branch of the Federal government as they are demanding?

Likewise, the proliferation of Russia's military build-up and the painful task of recruiting enough military personnel to maintain minimum strength in our all-volunteer Armed Forces is causing thoughtful consideration of bringing back the draft. The number of men and women in uniform has declined 40 percent in the last ten years[5] even though by 1978, some 130,000 women—more than 6 percent of the forces—are expected to be in uniform. But according to General Alexander M. Haig, Jr., supreme allied commander of Europe, the Soviets have added about one million men to their forces in the same time span.[6]

In a letter to Congressman Olin Teague, dated January 13, 1977, the Controller General of the U.S. stated: "The Department of State views the [IWY] Commission as a means to carry out international programs within the Secretary's authority to conduct foreign affairs."

Is our Department of State also committed to general and complete disarmament—like IWY—whether Russia disarms or not?

Where do IWY's sympathies lie? In one breath, the Commission votes to "ratify ERA at the earliest possible moment" knowing full well that it will force women to be drafted and serve in combat while encouraging its own daughters to be conscientious objectors. In the next breath, supposedly carrying out views of the U.S. State Department, it calls for total disarmament, with an unfriendly United Nations as the only protection against hostilities by a potential U.S. assailant!

Is this philosophy the spirit of antichrist? And is it moving the earth toward the prophesied One World Dictator? How far down the road of humanism will feminists take us under the guise of "equal rights"?

Already farther than many fancied. Sgt. Ann Sandeven, a 16-year veteran roughing it for the first time, explains: "We're living in the woods in tents. We're digging our own latrines and hauling our own fuel and water.

"There are some men who are trying to make us women do work we're not capable of doing," she said of the first major field test for women during NATO war games in West Germany. "We shouldn't be forced to do this just because Women's Liberation started the equality movement."

Without a doubt, these pilot programs are designed to prepare the military for possible ratification of the Equal Rights Amendment. G.I. Jill, indeed!

Trust in God, *She'll* Provide

"Because...when they knew God, they glorified him not as God, neither were thankful; but became vain in their imaginations, and their foolish heart was darkened."— Romans 1:21.

The glaring lights dimmed and the anchorwoman stood up, exchanging good-humored banter with the weatherman. The evening television newscast was over. As we unfastened our neck microphones, I turned to my "face off" opponent and asked, "Now be honest—if you are really for equal rights, don't you think my nonfeminist viewpoint ought to have some representation on the 59-member Illinois International Women's Year Coordinating Committee? After all, the IWY has $100,000 of everyone's Federal tax dollars to spend in our state."

"No," replied the local NOW president without hesitation. "Why should you as long as your churches have tax-exempt status? They are not helping pay for social programs so my taxes are really subsidizing your churches!"

I was not surprised by her answer, because she admittedly embraced humanism. Her response was the typical attitude of many feminists with whom I had been matched on radio, television, college campuses and before church and civic groups from one end of the state to the other.

A university professor had been even more bold. She freely admitted, while our TV talk-show was still on the air, that churches should lose their tax-exempt status if they refused to ordain women. This attack on denominations which condone so-called "sexism" is the national policy of NOW. In addition, feminists demand that homosexuals and lesbians be given equal rights to ordination in order for churches to retain special tax advantage.

This is not idle talk among fringe radicals. Many constitutional authorities believe the Equal Rights Amendment would further chisel away at our freedom of worship. Opinions are based on Supreme Court decisions regarding Bob Jones University[1] in South Carolina, and Bobbes Private School and Fairfax-Brewster School in Virginia.[2] They involved rulings that religious or private schools may not discriminate on the basis of race without losing tax-exempt status. Thus a new precedent may have been set undermining separation of church and state.

How has America come so far from the beliefs of those who fled to the New World for religious freedom? Christopher Columbus wrote, "It was the Lord who put into my mind to sail from here to the Indies. . . .The fact that the Gospel must still be preached to so many lands in such a short time—this is what convinces me." The very cornerstone of our heritage was penned at Plymouth Rock in the Mayflower Compact: "In the name of God, Amen."

Puritans, Catholics, Quakers and Jews all sought liberty to worship God according to the dictates of their hearts. So important was this issue to the framers of our Constitution that the Bill of Rights listed as the very first Amendment: "Congress shall make no law respecting establishment of religion, or prohibiting the free exercise thereof. . ."

83

Two centuries later—spawned by humanism—Women's Lib, with the axe of apostasy, hacks away at the faith of our founding fathers. With the blessings of the National Council of Churches, two feminists prepared a "Guide to Nonsexist Interpretation of the Bible." It questions the propriety of referring to God as Father and Jesus as He, wondering when the Holy Spirit will become She. And the writers insist that women striving for Biblical equality use both feminine and masculine metaphors to denote God.

"If God is a *humanist*," Ms. Letty Russell says, "then surely, using contemporary language, God is a *feminist*."[3]

No wonder state representative Thomas Hanahan (Ill.-D.), in voting against the Equal Rights Amendment, exclaimed in a radio interview, "These women even want to change the Lord's Prayer to our *Mother* who art in Heaven!"

"Beware of false prophets, who come to you in sheep's clothing. Inwardly they are ravening wolves," Jesus warned His disciples. "By their fruits ye shall know them" (Matthew 7:15, 20).

IWY delegates and supporters at the National Women's Conference proclaimed their true affinities, waving banners "Jesus was a Feminist," "Ordain Women or Stop Baptizing Them," and "Trust in God, *She'll* Provide." But there was one nonfeminist sign which Kansas Pro-Family delegate Barbara Jefferies felt summed up the entire weekend proceedings: "Jesus Wept."

Pressure on our churches and synagogues to accept feminist demands has been building since the National Organization for Women was founded in 1966, as an outgrowth of commissions on the status of women. As early as 1972, NOW national board member Mary Jean Collins—who served as program chairperson for Illinois' IWY Women's Meeting—was marching in a candlelight protest against Protestant, Catholic and Jewish faiths which allegedly discriminate against women.

By 1975, NOW's national convention in Philadelphia advocated a renewed and more intense campaign against the Roman Catholic church and increased support for homosexuals. It was the year NOW joined with the National Women's

Agenda in promoting goals of the United Nations International Women's Year conference held in Mexico City that June.

Congresswoman Bella Abzug—later to become U.S. IWY chairperson—explained the Agenda in the December 1975, *Ms.* magazine, published and edited by Patricia Carbine and Gloria Steinem who have both served as IWY commissioners:

"The Agenda signals the beginning of what can be an activist coalition embracing women from such diverse groups as YWCA, Girl's Clubs of America, League of Women Voters, National Women's Political Caucus, Church Women United, Campfire Girls. . .National Council of Jewish Women. . . National Gay Task Force. . ." Ms. Abzug wrote. "The Agenda is significant, not only because of the demands it makes, but because it establishes the minimum objectives for change. . .

"The next step will be a national conference of women that will have an opportunity to debate, change, modify, expand and ultimately ratify a women's agenda," she predicted. "A House subcommittee has unanimously passed my bill, cosponsored by fourteen Congresswomen, to appropriate Federal funds for conventions of American women to be held next year."

The asking price was ten million dollars; Congress reduced Ms. Abzug's request to a five-million-dollar pittance!

The demands were preceded by a preamble which concluded: "The U.S. National Women's Agenda declares full equality under law, as embodied in the Equal Rights Amendment, to be essential to the equality of opportunity and access for women in all aspects of life, including specifically:

• Elimination of sex role, racial and cultural stereotyping at every level of the educational system

• Inclusion of realistic curricula on health and human sexuality throughout the education process

• Removal of sex bias from the Social Security system and introduction of coverage for unpaid homemakers

• Comprehensive revision of family laws

• Creation of a comprehensive and adequate system of child care

• Implementation of the legal right of women to control their own reproductive systems

• Extension of all civil rights legislation to prohibit discrimination based on affectional or sexual preference.

Why did these religious organizations commit their memberships to support anti-Scriptural agenda items which later became part of the IWY's National Plan of Action? Marilyn Johnson, an American Lutheran Church (ALC) pastor's wife, wrote me of an astonishing discovery within her own denomination that shows how "false prophets" have crept into churches.

Mrs. Johnson, a registered nurse and mother of four sons, dropped in on some sessions of a Sexual Attitude Reassessment (SAR) program, funded in part and directed by ministers of her church. SAR had been developed by the University of Minnesota Medical School in cooperation with the ALC's theological ethical task force. Playboy Foundation had supported this sexual misadventure with a gift of $45,000. Its initial thrust was to "help" professional people—Lutheran seminary students, clergy and social service workers—who counsel others.

What she found was a brainwashing "desensitizing sexorama" where participants were bombarded with explicit films projected simultaneously on the walls—heterosexual intercourse, homosexual sex, masturbation, bestiality and masochism—while blaring rock music pulsated through the room. On display were erotic merchandise, artificial sex organs, vibrators and other articles she did not even know existed.

A self-avowed gay minister led a session on homosexuality arguing that "people ought to be free to do anything they want sexually so long as it does not exploit other people's rights."

One exercise dealt with "values clarification" in which participants evaluated their mores regarding sexual behavior. By the end of the sessions, many found they tended toward a liberal outlook.

"It is a diabolical and subversive movement to undermine the moral values of our society!" Marilyn exclaimed. "It is contrary to Christian belief. We know this, because when you come into the course you are told that 'sexuality must be understood apart from morality or it really can't be understood at all.' The promoters of SAR say, 'Christianity is crippling.

You have sexual hangups if you feel responsibility toward God's law.' They feel that if you can do away with God's law, then you won't feel guilty about the things that you might want to do sexually. If you can get a church to endorse it, then you're giving it legitimacy and respectability, which you would not otherwise have."

Mrs. Johnson began to ask herself, "What can I do about it?"

She organized a Family Rights group and set up a speakers' bureau to inform other Christians. "Seminarians are being encouraged to take the course. Now if you can get them conditioned to accept this kind of sexuality and they go out into parishes and teach accordingly, what will happen to the morals of America?

"Church people, being trusting and uninformed, don't want to be discriminators," she admits. "So the church is a target for homosexuals. That effort has filtered from national church conferences (Methodist and Presbyterian, for example) which have produced study papers calling for 'tolerance for and legalization of homosexuality.'"

Ultimately, her efforts prevented an entire community from being "desensitized."

"When they contacted our speakers' bureau and we were able to tell them that two homosexuals would be conducting SAR, it created quite a furor. Mabel, Minnesota, had had a homosexual living in their town who had been abusing young fellows for a number of years before it was brought to light. The last thing parents wanted was for a couple of gays to come in and tell their children that this was a normal alternate lifestyle."

Don't be complacent if you're not Lutheran. The *PTA* magazine of September 1974, carried an article in praise of SAR, co-authored by the minister who directs it!

Like Catholics United for the Faith and Good News Methodists, Presbyterians for Scriptural Faith have joined the battle against this "falling away." Writing in the *Presbyterian Layman,* professor of history Richard Lovelace at Gordon-Conwell Theological Seminary traces this pagan attack on the church back to apostolic days:

"Much of our current ethical thinking is wholly man-centered; it asks only if an act is agreeable to the human being involved, and ignores the question of whether God is pleased with what is done. . .But it is highly significant that the apostles do not let down the barriers to accommodate themselves to pagan sexual mores, which tolerated fornication, adultery, and homosexual acts with little public stigma.

"Instead, Paul indicates that one of the major signs of the religious bankruptcy of paganism is the helpless tendency of its intellectual leaders toward sexual inversion. Homosexuality and lesbianism are listed first after idolatry in the catalog of depravity in Romans 1:18-32 because they are the warning signs that a violation of reason and nature has occurred. Men have inverted God's order by worshipping the creature rather than the Creator. . ."

Why, in spite of Scriptural abhorrence of this "alternate lifestyle," are many denominations backing the ERA in which legality of homosexual marriage is implicit? And why has this perversion become a women's rights issue?

"You've come a long way, baby," Lucifer says to contemporary Eves.

The Salem Children's Home in Illinois had a different dose of equal rights administered by a "Women's Libber deluxe" inspecting for use of Federal child welfare funds under the Affirmative Action Program. My friend, Fern Kipfer, whose husband serves on the board of directors, brought me the checklist of government interventions—five single-spaced pages of them.

The home and farm is run by the Evangelical Mennonite Church, yet the reviewer insisted that there is no exception allowed for religious "discrimination" under Title VII of the 1964 Civil Rights Act.

"Specified religious beliefs, attitudes and practices may not be required of employees or residents," she wrote. (Employment qualifications including a definite experience of salvation and a willingness to work in harmony with the church would have to go.)

"Reinforcement of sex role stereotyping which limits and distorts self-concepts and life options" like "girls do their own ironing; boys do not. . .boys have access to farm work; girls do not" is illegal for religious institutions receiving Federal funds.

It is not difficult to understand how tax-exempt status of churches, parochial schools and religious organizations soon may evaporate. Feminist lawyer Florynce Kennedy, who says, "Women like Phyllis Schlafly should be slapped around," has already launched a suit to deprive the Catholic church of its tax-exempt status.

Parade magazine suggested on February 13, 1977, that initiatives could be made that would create a background for rational debate for rescinding tax exemptions for religious charitable purposes. "One [initiative] would require the periodic preparation and publication of accurate and complete information on exempt property," the article hinted.

The Charity Disclosure Bill (HR41) was introduced in the U.S. House within the year!

"Does HR 41 presage the further erosion of religious freedom?" the National Association of Evangelicals asks. "It would allow the U.S. Postal Service to get control of financial records—expense accounts, contributors lists, etc.—to verify that the religious organization is publishing honest figures."

NAE is concerned that the bill violates the First Amendment, separating church and state by government regulation of church activities. And, of course, it implies that all religious groups are guilty of attempting to swindle the public.

"Here is the latest—I have been liberated, like it or not," writes the wife of a college ministry couple on staff at the University of Toledo. "The government has required Campus Crusade to issue *separate* checks to husbands and wives!"

The overwhelming effect of combined humanist/feminist infiltration of church policy became readily apparent to a Christian gentleman who had long been active in his major denomination's affairs.

"We have a husband and wife team who are both ministers at our church," he told me recently. "She is a feminist and is always promoting Women's Lib ideas from the pulpit."

Unfortunately, when my friend shared his concerns with a church official, he was told, "You'd better keep quiet or you'll get a homosexual next time!"

The vice moderator of the United Church of Christ, the Rev. Donna Schaper, was an observer at the National Women's Conference. "We are concerned about those who identify themselves as religious but misquote the Bible. Somehow they claim that the Bible says we must obey Christ and obey our husbands—that's outrageous," Ms. Schaper said. "The people who wrote the Bible lived in an historic time, and just because people then put down the gays doesn't mean we have to do so today."

Even Sister Margaret Traxler, a delegate-at-large and former president of the Coalition of American Nuns, told reporters she, too, supported both the sexual preference and abortion resolutions. "There's no doubt that Roman Catholic bishops feel they have the right to pontificate about women's bodies," she said.[4] (In May 1978, U.S. bishops refused to endorse ERA because of its possible adverse effects on the family and its link to abortion.)

This hostility to God's Word was exemplified in all its ugliness following a talk I gave on the National Women's Conference where I displayed Women's Lib materials including the bumper sticker, "Trust in God, *She'll* Provide." Even though a Catholic bishop, a priest and two Baptist ministers were seated at the speaker's table with me, a feminist asked me, "Why shouldn't we call God 'she?' How do you know if God has a penis?"

An audible gasp rippled through the large audience.

"Jesus Christ was born of a Virgin, died on the cross for our sins, and then rose from the grave that we might have eternal life if we accept His gift," I said. "If someone with those credentials calls God 'Father,' then that's good enough for me!"

In her book *Marching Orders for the End Battle,* Corrie Ten Boom says, "Every Christian is involved in this battle, whether he wants it or not. . . .We can shut our eyes to the danger and not see where the course of world history will lead us. But Jesus says , 'Watch ye, therefore, and pray always. . . .'."

Miss Ten Boom, a victim of Nazi concentration camps for hiding Jews from the Gestapo, encourages believers to "know our enemy. . . .We cannot escape the war by looking for another front line."

Women's Lib, American Style

*". . .the Conferences will provide a forum for
people of opposing views. . ."—Bella Abzug*

Saturday mall shoppers jiggled the television camera lights
on their spindly metal stands as curious onlookers crowded
around Senator Charles H. Percy's "listen-in" table. As I waited my turn to speak with the senator, I counted forty Eagle
Forum, Right to Life, STOP ERA and Birthright members I
had alerted earlier that morning. They were carrying clever
handmade signs.

"Rosemary Thomson," a downstate aide called.

I stepped forward, a stack of press releases and International
Women's Year publications on one arm, and shook hands
with the smiling lawmaker. The TV cameras began to roll.
From behind, newscasters from area radio stations pushed

91

tape-recorder "mikes" between us.

The senator paused. "They are recording us. Do you mind?"

"She asked us to come!" a female reporter put in.

I handed Percy and members of the press a prepared copy of my complaint. After pointing out that the Illinois IWY Coordinating Committee, with $100,000 Federal tax dollars to spend on a women's conference in our state, was made up of five pro-ERA female legislators and many members of NOW, the Women's Political Caucus, the Status of Women Commission and other feminist groups, I asked,

"Senator Percy, how can you be for 'equal rights' and serve on both the national and state IWY when only one of Illinois' 59 committee members represents the traditional values upheld by the organizations I represent here today?"

With his answer being recorded on tape and film, the lawmaker remained pleasant. "I agree that your movement is strong here. You have succeeded in stopping the ERA, and you should have representation. If there is no other way to do it, I'll step down from my seat—there are many others who can express my opinion—and give it up to someone from your group." That evening, two television stations carried Senator Percy's complete answer to my question. He was now committed. And Christian women who had taken time to act on their convictions had scored a small victory against Women's Lib domination of the coming June IWY conference.

Or so we thought.

It was February 1977. The first of 56 state and territorial International Women's Year Conferences had just been held in Vermont. A one-day "trial run," the Vermont Women's Town Meeting, confirmed the misgiving of Pro-Family/Pro-Life advocates who had begged Congress not to give five million dollars to the presidentially appointed National Commission on the Observance of International Women's Year to sponsor these events. Attorney Nellie Gray, president of March for Life, had flown from Washington, D.C., to observe Vermont's activities after Right to Lifers learned of the conference from a brief news article only one week prior to the conclave. Miss Gray—along with Elaine Donnelly and Jill Ulbrich of Ohio Eagle Forum—earlier had testified before the

U.S. House Appropriations Committee against the funding of IWY conferences because they suspected the meetings would be used to promote abortion-on-demand and the deceptive ERA. The outcome of Vermont's conference added an additional anti-Christian category: gay rights!

Because resolutions emanating from these conferences were supposed to express "grass roots" opinions of each state, the tactics of the Vermont IWY coordinating committee were even more shocking since the results would be submitted to state and Federal legislators for enactment into law! It was evident to Nellie and Vermonters Marie Dietz and Casey Norris that Pro-Life/Pro-Family sentiment was not wanted by the coordinators. Actions demonstrated a calculated attempt to circumvent congressional intent that concerns of women from all walks of life be discussed. Parliamentary procedure was ignored, preventing consideration of all issues. Rules fluctuated at the whim of the committee, and the unfair election process to select delegates to the National IWY Conference polled 12 pro-ERA, pro-abortion, pro-lesbian winners; 0 traditional women.

After extensive correspondence with the National Commission protesting the conduct of Vermont's IWY, Miss Norris— a licensed engineer—wrote with tongue-in-cheek, "I think I've arrived! Now even Bella herself (or is it hr.self?) writes to me, but I remain unintimidated, unimpressed. . .and unanswered. She is perfectly satisfied with their actions, but what can we expect when the wolf is asked to mind the chickens?"

The Vermont IWY was a sample of things to come. In March, Kathryn Dunaway, a "token" member of the Georgia coordinating committee, received a packet from IWY's national chairman entitled "core" recommendations. Based on the anti-family results of the first state conference and similar endorsements in the IWY policy manual ". . .To Form a More Perfect Union. . .," the Commission had condensed all their radical feminist goals into 16 proposals which the remaining conferences were expected to approve.

Mrs. Dunaway, 70-year-old dynamo who heads Georgia's STOP ERA, phoned me immediately.

"Rosemary, this is terrible! We've got to warn Christians in other states that IWY plans to 'railroad' these Women's Lib resolutions through all the meetings and then tell Congress and the President that the majority of women want these laws!" she said.

Also included in the "core" agenda were recommendations that homemakers receive Social Security in their own right instead of through their husbands' benefits; international interdependence replacing national sovereignty; equal quotas of men and women in employment, elective and appointive office; and universal child care sponsored by the Federal government.

And so it was that the IWY Citizens' Review Committee was formed with myself as national chairman and Nellie Gray, Elaine Donnelly, Kathryn Dunaway, two state legislators and other like-minded women on the advisory board. We passed the word to leaders in churches and Pro-Family/Pro-Life organizations, encouraging them to become involved in their own IWY conferences. Although the official Coordinating Committees in each state offered themselves as a "balanced" slate to be elected to the National Women's Conference, our coalition often turned out in sufficient numbers to nominate women of our persuasion from the floor, and actually elected around 20 percent of the total delegation nationally. By thwarting the dictatorial tactics of some states' coordinators, we demonstrated that not all U.S. women desire feminist-oriented goals.

The second state meeting fell on Mother's Day weekend in Georgia. To assess the tactics of IWY policymakers firsthand, I attended and, at the same time, kicked-off the formation of our coalition. By this time, we had discovered that *all* state committees were made up of one narrow viewpoint with an anti-ERA or Pro-Life member as a "token" of balanced representation. These committees reflected the bias of the women who had appointed them—the National IWY—a virtual Who's Who of feminist/lesbian activists serving interchangeably on the boards of NOW, the National Women's Political Caucus (NWPC), the National Gay Rights Task Force (NGTF) and other pro-ERA/pro-abortion groups. At the outset, I shared this information with the media at our Citizens' Review press conference, predicting the results of the two-day confab in advance.

"You have no business interviewing anyone without our permission!" an irate IWY official told one female TV reporter in an open effort to suppress the facts.

"As a member of the working press, I have a right to talk with whomever I choose," was the reporter's indignant response. And she chose to air, on both evening newscasts, IWY's attempt to control public information.

As the conference progressed, I knew that reports from Vermont had not been exaggerated. Panelists in the Education Workshop promoted Federal child *development*—day care plus nutrition, mental and physical health and education as a "right" of parenthood. Two Christian ladies decided to see what the Sexual Orientation Workshop was about. They made a prompt retreat upon entering a roomful of lesbians who were patting each other's bodies and calling out dirty names. (Incidentally after President Carter named Bella Abzug as new IWY chair and ex-nun Jean O'Leary, National Gay Rights co-chair, to the National Commission early in 1977, a discussion of homosexual rights became required criteria for all meetings. Minnesota held 25 lesbian-type workshops, and Hawaii's shocking program, "What Lesbians Do," was "entertainment.") The Health Care Workshop gave information on a variety of health problems until—near the conclusion—a resolution promoting abortion was sprung, complete with a roving clique of abortion proponents who entered the session just in time to vote and pass the measure which had never been discussed!

Even though Georgia's women's meeting was financed by the U.S. government, there had been no invocation, no pledge to the flag, indeed, no American flag in sight! A somewhat dubious prayer was offered by a female clergyperson at the Friday banquet that began: "Our Creator who nurtures us like a mother. . ." Bella Abzug's after-dinner speech showed the open disaffection that feminists have for men—including God as a father-figure. Instead of celebrating the advancement of women, Ms. Abzug charged that American females

95

were mere chattel, continually put-upon by a conspiratorial male-dominated society. Open cardboard boxes to hold ballots of "core" recommendations were left unattended in the hotel lobby, making vote fraud a temptation if not a fact.

Because of our Citizens' Review Committee alert, Georgia did elect three Christian delegates and one alternate to represent women of traditional moral values at the NWC. The climax came, however, when the final general session defeated a resolution offered by our coalition asking that textbooks in the public school reflect the moral and religious values of parents. Dozens of women walked out in protest and tears.

"The IWY has just used our own tax money to cast a vote against God," sobbed one visibly shaken mother.

The story of Georgia's conference was repeated in state after state through July, with God-fearing homemakers and career women left in shock and outrage at the way a governmental committee got by with such inveigling manipulation. The Equal Rights Amendment workshop of Illinois' IWY was a clear-cut case of devious methods and probably a violation of the law prohibiting use of Federal funds to lobby.

I received a phone call from one of the Illinois coordinators in early May. "Would you like to be a panelist for the ERA Workshop?"

"I'd like to know the ground rules and who the other panelists are. Will an equal number represent each side?" I inquired.

"Oh, this is not a debate! There will be someone in favor of ERA and a legal opinion," she said evasively.

"That certainly doesn't sound like equal rights to me. After all, there are legal opinions both for and against the amendment," I pointed out. "And while we're talking about the program, I wonder if IWY will be having any other nonfeminists speaking in different workshops. You know, a member of Citizens' Review personally handed your program chairman a suggested list of speakers in April. She claims to have lost it and I submitted another but have heard nothing."

The caller hesitated. "Well, I don't have anything to do with the rest of the program. I couldn't tell you."

This chicanery was typical of the treatment our women had been receiving. Of nearly 50 panelists, paid $50 each from the Federal grant, I was the only Pro-Family woman! The way we were able to get any information about Illinois IWY plans was through an anti-ERA friend who had been inadvertently named to the coordinating committee. She had provided me with the official committee minutes which stated that only organizations belonging to the Illinois Women's Agenda were selected for advance mailings. It was a deliberate shut-out of opposing views.

The caller, whom I knew to be a paid ERA lobbyist, continued, "I'll get back to you on the format."

Three days prior to the June 11 workshop, I was still waiting to hear how the panel was to be conducted or even how long I would speak, in spite of numerous efforts to get the details. Finally, I called our family attorney, a personal friend, and explained the situation.

"Jim," I concluded, "our coalition has no money to pay you, but I need you to go with me."

"We have a family reunion planned for that day." He paused. "But this is a moral obligation. I'll go."

By 1:30 Saturday afternoon, all the seats in Hayden Auditorium on Illinois State University's campus were taken. Lawyer Cummings and I approached the platform where a number of IWY officials were gathered.

"We want to know what the rules are going to be here," Jim demanded of the National IWY commissioner, who was to be the moderator, and the legal counsel from Washington, D.C.

"Each panelist will get ten minutes," they responded.

"I assume that Mrs. Thomson and Ms. Peters listed here in the program are the only speakers?" he asked, scrutinizing the pro-ERA assemblege on the stage.

"Oh, no!" The moderator smiled sweetly. "Sister Mary Rehmann, a law student, will give a legal opinion."

"That's not fair!" Jim's voice was courtroom stern. "I insist on equal time for my client."

"Mrs. Thomson is welcome to invite someone else to speak against the ERA if she likes," the moderator condescended.

I could hardly believe my ears! I had asked for that privilege a month before, but IWY coordinators had refused to answer my letters and phone calls. Finally, the legal counsel decided to give each proponent 10 minutes; I would have 20 minutes. Ironically, the official timekeeper, president of Illinois Men for ERA, was seated *behind* the podium with a wrist watch so no one knew when time was up.

The moderator introduced those seated on stage. There were the female legal counsel, a second national commissioner, two members of the Illinois IWY committee, the timekeeper—all ERA advocates—in addition to the pantsuited nun and the NOW/WPC lobbyist who was the workshop coordinator and now my opposing panelist. Jim and I were the only con representatives even though the Illinois General Assembly had defeated the Equal Rights Amendment for five years consecutively.

Ms. Peters spoke first. Applause. During my presentation, hoots and jeers forced the moderator to ask for quiet from ERA backers. Sister Rehmann then gave a quasi-legal/religious dissertation.

"According to Federal law governing this conference," I reminded the moderator, "religion is specifically not to be discussed."

"Oh, that simply means we can't have an entire workshop in religion," she explained away the infraction. (Yet, no one had adequately explained why Virginia was allowed to have a Women and Spirituality session—on witchcraft led by witches!)

To conclude the "equal" agenda, the moderator gave a lengthy pitch for ERA using Old Testament Scripture. She suggested that civil law is synonymous with God creating "them"—man and woman—with spiritual equality, while ignoring the important differences of legal equality.

Almost immediately, a state female legislator in the audience made a motion to endorse ERA. Response against a vote without discussion from nearly 500 participants indicated STOP ERA'ers were in the majority. Discourse began. But in the back of the auditorium, a member of Citizens' Review overheard an interesting exchange between the lawmaker and the workshop "facilitator" who directs a NOW activist training center in Chicago, financed in part by Federal grants.

"They are three-fourths opposed. What'll we do about that?" the representative inquired.

The "facilitator" whispered a response, and the legislator left the room. Before long, young women with ERA YES voting cards began entering the hall, completely blocking all aisles as they sat on the floor. (I learned later they had been recruited from another workshop with the plea, "ERA is in trouble. Get over there right away.") A member of the audience called the moderator's attention to the rule adopted that morning prohibiting those entering late from voting.

"We'll put everyone on their honor," she said. "If you arrived late, please don't vote."

But when the question was called, everyone voted. Needless to say, ERA was "enthusiastically endorsed" by a slim margin! A registered parliamentarian in the audience asked to be heard; someone else called for a recount.

"Hurry up and adjourn this meeting," a proponent directed the moderator.

She rapped the gavel. The "railroading" operation came to an end.

Departing participants received two handouts. One was a "hate" list describing Pro-Family/Pro-Life nominees for national delegates as "enemies of women's rights." I was one of them. The other paper contained names of state legislators who voted against ERA, with instructions to picket their homes on Father's Day. What could be more plainly construed as using the IWY conference to lobby? Especially when representatives observed ERA leaders attending the workshop marching in front of their homes the following Sunday. (In Illinois, picketing a home is illegal, anyway.)

The week after our IWY fiasco, I had a call from Arizona. "Have you heard of MMOPP? The implementors move from one workshop to another to make sure IWY's Reproductive Freedom (abortion) and ERA resolutions are passed. Tucson's Women's Political Caucus was behind it here."

"No, but I certainly saw the plan in action in Georgia and Illinois!"

Senator Jesse Helms' office had been in touch with me several times regarding the unfair activities of IWY. I dialed

Sarah Simms, an intern for Helms, and explained MMOPP.

"Sarah," I asked, "can you locate any documentation on this? It might be coming out of the national WPC headquarters."

The next day Miss Simms called back. "I have a copy of MMOPP. It is four pages on NWPC letterhead. At least eleven of their board members are on the National IWY Commission including Bella Abzug, the national president of the League of Women Voters, the chairwoman of ERAmerica, Jean O' Leary and Gloria Steinem!"

"How did you get it?"

"I went right down to the NWPC office here in D.C.!"

The directive had gone to the chairman of every state WPC. (The Illinois IWY chairman was *also* the chair of the WPC, and the legislator who set the plan in motion in our ERA workshop is a WPC member.) Monitoring and Mobile Operation Partnership Program (MMOPP) gave specific techniques for defrauding Pro-Life/anti-ERA participants at state conferences. The conclusion was direct: "A number of potentially friendly people thought our tactics were too blunt and maybe even unfair. . .NEVER GIVE YOUR ENEMY AN EVEN BREAK." (Emphasis in original.)

In the weeks that followed, Senator Helms compiled the most blatant cases of violations and biases from reports I had received from around the country. Introducing his finding into the *Congressional Record* on July 12, the senator charged: "Enough information has come to light to reveal a widespread pattern and practice of discrimination by IWY and its state affiliates against those who do not agree with the narrow and negative ideology and partisan biases of IWY organizers. . . . Reports indicate rigged sessions, handpicked committees, stacked registration and little or no publicity to women at large. . . .The IWY program represents a violation of the rights of all women who believe in the social and moral values of womanhood."

It was for these reasons that Senator Helms arranged ad hoc hearings to bring to public and congressional attention the breach of spirit of Public Law 94-167 granting IWY five million dollars. This action was prompted by the refusal of

Representative Tom Steed (D.-Okla.), subcommittee chairman of the House Appropriations Committee, to investigate protests of traditional women as requested by Congressman Robert Michel. Two days of testimony laid bare the feminist collusion to promote their own goals at taxpayers' expense!

I exposed MMOPP, while Darlene Dagenhardt—a longtime Illinois election official—expressed concern over balloting for delegates to the National Women's Conference: "There is no such thing as an honest election when candidates or their representatives are not permitted to observe counting of ballots. I fear this may have set a dangerous precedent for future Federally funded elections."

Mary Tracey told of repeated attempts to get registration forms for Pro-Life New Yorkers. Six weeks later, when it was too late for family women to make plans to be away from home for a weekend, the forms arrived. "Get your own funds and have your own conference," an IWY official told her.

"A perfect illustration of how one-sided the Wisconsin conference was," Reny Liebner told Congressmen, "is that the *Chicago Sun Times* thought it was funded by NOW."

"I want to explode a common myth about women—that they cannot keep a secret," protested Marie Dietz regarding lack of publicity for Vermont's IWY.

"I would like to leave you with this picture. . .hundreds of purple armbanded lesbians. . .with gestures of clenched fist defiance. . .posters and tables of lesbian, socialist and marxist literature. . .workshops on revolution and sex, including one on oral sodomy by a counselor in the Sexual Attitudes Reassessment program. . . .A horrifying picture traditional family women will never forget," Minnesota Eagle Forum chairman Terry Todd related.

"One Pennsylvania Sexuality Workshop discussed necrophilia," Eithne Mary Hartnet reported. "Do you know what that is? Making love with a corpse!"

Businesswoman Betty Hanicke declared, "The most blatant abuse of Kansas IWY chairman's power was the lock-out of Pro-Life/anti-ERA women from the General Plenary Session."

"California displayed unique equipment—masturbating wands, vibrators, and speculums for self-examination. One pregnant woman looking at abortion devices was offered instruction on how to perform an abortion on herself!" narrated Mary Schmitz, shocking even the press.

"Why did my tax money go toward the showing of a porno performance featuring the sex acts of deviates?" asked Helen Priester, owner of a Waikiki gift shop. "This culminated with two lesbians making love together on stage in a pay toilet!"

In a few states—Oklahoma, Utah, Hawaii, Mississippi, Alabama, Montana, Ohio, Missouri, Indiana and Nebraska—Pro-Family participants outnumbered Women's Lib factions, electing nonfeminist delegates. And IWY officials expressed "outrage" that these delegations were "unfairly balanced" despite the fact that 80 percent of those chosen for Houston's NWC adhered to IWY goals!

Was it an accident that International Women's Year activities had been so openly biased? I doubt it, considering that Percy ignored his televised promise to the women of Illinois— to insure Pro-Life/anti-ERA representation on our IWY Coordinating Committee. For as co-keynoter with Bella Abzug at our IWY meeting, the senator spoke in favor of Women's Lib objectives!

"If the intent of Congress was to establish a forum whereby the feminist movement could undermine the home, the family, religion and our very democracy," Jacquline Sumner of Iowa speculated at the ad hoc hearings, "then, gentlemen, you have succeeded beyond your wildest dreams."

Mexico City—a Blueprint

"...and this is the spirit of antichrist of which you have heard..."—I John 4:3

"Mr. Chairman and members of the committee, International Women's Year's most serious offense is that—according to its own material—'what women want' never was intended to be part of the IWY conferences in the United States. The goals of IWY were written in June 1975, when the United Nations held its world conference of the International Women's Year in Mexico City, Mexico. It was there that the World Plan of Action for the Implementation of the Objectives of the International Women's Year[1] was unanimously adopted," began Jill Ulbrich, soft-spoken mother of two, in testimony before Senator Jesse Helms' ad hoc hearings. "According to a U.S. State Department bulletin, 'The Plan provides guidelines

103

for national action over the 10-year period from 1975 to 1985 as part of a sustained, long-term effort to achieve the objectives of the International Women's Year.'

"Mr. Chairman, the World Plan does not set guidelines to allow American women to decide the goals of IWY. Those goals were predetermined for us!"

It was September 14, 1977. The third floor caucus room of the Russell Senate Office Building was astir with news reporters, a CBS-TV crew, and more than 200 women from 42 states, some with infants in strollers.

Several hours earlier, the proceedings had begun with the presentation of an orchid lei to Senator Helms by Mrs. Priester. She, like the entire delegation of concerned Christian women, had paid her own air fare to Washington, D.C., to share with Congress the traditional women's assessment of the stormy IWY women's meetings.

Mrs. Ulbrich, a Dayton, Ohio, Sunday School teacher, continued, "The World Plan concerns itself with how to implement these predetermined goals. Page 26 of the bulletin states: 'The monitoring of trends and policies relating to women and relevant to their plan of action should be undertaken continuously. . .beginning in 1978. Such monitoring would focus mainly on new and emerging trends and policies.' Mr. Chairman, what will the 'new and emerging trends and policies' be? Who will determine them for us?"

The U.S. International Women's Year state conferences, culminating in the National Women's Conference in Houston, Texas, November 19-22, 1977, were an outgrowth of this UN-IWY world conference. The World Plan of action is a strange conglomeration of objectives covering virtually every area of the lives of men, women and children, although the publicly stated goals are "equality, development and peace."

The intent of this plan gets quickly to the point in its early paragraphs: "The developing countries, which account for 70 percent of the population of the world, receive only 30 percent of the world income. . . .For this reason, it is urgent to implement a new international economic order. . . .In our times, women's role will increasingly emerge as a powerful revolutional social force. . . ."

Considering that present U.S. economy is based on private free enterprise, the alternative—or new economic order—would necessarily be socialism: government ruling people rather than government of, by and for the people. Our system is most compatible with Christian values because it allows each individual his or her free choice. The Declaration of Independence set the philosophy of our government, inscribing that "all men are created equal, that they are endowed by their Creator with certain inalienable rights, that among these are life, liberty, and the pursuit of happiness. . ."

Those fifty-six patriots who wrote and signed this unique document affirmed God is our Creator, and we are made in His image, with a free will. They declared each person is equal before God. Not born equal. Not made equal by government. But gloriously equal in God's sight, in His love for us; yet different—unequal, if you will—in every way from every other human being.

"From the day of the Declaration," John Adams alleged, "they, the Americans, were bound by the laws of God which they all [acknowledge], and by the laws of the Gospel, which they nearly all acknowledge as the rules of their conduct."

Socialism, on the other hand, sees no supernatural end for man, no soul needing salvation. Socialism believes mankind will be regenerated by altering the environment, and putting men into the services of the State—which evolves into an earthly paradise. Therefore, a new economic order needs a secular religion to sanction its authoritarian politics, replacing the traditional moral order by a scheme subordinating individuals to the State. The planners view humans as a mass, denying their full stature with rights endowed by the Creator, gifted with free will, possessing the capacity to plan their own lives according to their own convictions.

IWY's twist to an old humanist idea is to require all women to play a major role in restructuring society into this world-wide socialistic system. Old and New Testament prophecies of a world government and an apostate religion ushering in a false peace are not difficult to imagine in light of the World Plan of Action. This proposed new society seems made-to-order for the world dictator of Revelation 13—antichrist.

The World Plan goes on to spell out IWY's goals with unbelievable frankness. "Equal Rights" is the rallying slogan for achieving this new social order, and is by the Plan's definition, equal responsibilities for women and men leading to "personal fulfillment and the benefit of society." It does not recognize that many women may not want equal responsibilities, and that personal fulfillment may take an entirely different route.

Very simply, God's plan for families is ignored. Not that He wants women to bury their capabilities. He wants to channel them. In His protective will, women are free to become all He intended, including developing creative talents which may lead to careers in or out of the home. This is the ideal way society benefits.

Nevertheless, IWY intends to change social attitudes through education to bring about the acceptance of shared responsibilities for home and children. This would create an "essential reassessment of the functions and roles traditionally allotted to each sex within the family. . . .In order to allow for women's equal (fuller) participation in all societal activities, socially organized services should be established. . .communal kitchens, and especially services for children should be provided."

In effect, the Plan is to put all women to work while the government provides child development centers "to supplement the training and care that the children get at home." It is a notion alien to Christian child-rearing (which charges parents with that responsibility) and ignores God's Commandment to "honor your father and mother. . ." not the State.

The equality concept includes the right of women to control their own bodies with regard to childbearing as "basic to the attainment of any real equality between the sexes." This, of course, is abortion-on-demand, and it is obvious why International Women's Year followed on the heels of the UN's World Population Plan of 1974, to "eliminate all social practices and legislative measures which discriminated on the grounds of sex. . ." Laws against abortion do discriminate against females.

Writing in *Today's Education,* Ms. Helvi Sipila, UN secretary general of IWY explained: "Everything done to increase the changes for women to have alternative choices in their lives to the traditional mother role will strengthen their capacity to make decisions about family size according to the best interest of their families and their countries. Thus, we see a clear relationship between the World Population Year, 1974, and International Women's Year, 1975."[2]

The primary objective of "development" is integrating women into the total job market. IWY wants women's contribution to society to be "more effective in terms of production" outside the home. "Full integration also implies that women receive their fair share of the benefits of development," the Plan asserts, "thereby helping to ensure a more equitable distribution of income among all sectors of the [world] population."

Nowhere could one find a better definition of socialism! This Utopia, by IWY rationale, will eliminate all sources of conflict because "true peace cannot be achieved unless women share with men the responsibility for establishing a new international economic order."

To the Christian who believes that only Christ can bring true peace both spiritually and on His return to reign on earth, the World Plan of Action takes on an ominous meaning. Does it signal the warning of I Thessalonians 5:3: "For when they shall say, peace and safety, then sudden destruction cometh upon them. . ."?

The meticulous details of implementing the World Plan include maximum use of mass communications media to change attitudes. Children's textbooks and teaching methods would be revised in conjunction with co-education classes to promote changes in attitudes. To ensure that women work, target dates would be established for substantial increases in the number of women employed; a reduction in working hours for men would provide more jobs for women; childcare facilities, maternity protection (insurance), maternity leaves, the right to return to former employment and nursing breaks would be guaranteed.

Have you wondered why television commercials now portray females as wives, mothers *and* working women? Why

107

public school textbooks no longer respect the moral and religious values of parents—as in the much-publicized government sponsored MACOS social studies series featuring graphic portrayals of wife-swapping, cannibalism, and the casual disposal of unwanted infants or the elderly?[3] Have you wondered about the logic of Title IX of the Federal Education Amendments that requires all classes to be co-educational? Or why "affirmative action" insists on the quota hiring of women? Or why the case for maternity benefits financed by employers was taken to the U.S. Supreme Court in 1977?

Speaking at a Midwest International Women's Year banquet in 1975, Chen Yaunchi, a citizen of the People's Republic of [Red] China, told YWCA members: "Women have to work in order to achieve economic independence. We learned that to achieve women's rights, we also need to have a drastic social change."

Ms. Yaunchi asserted that economic independence, political equality and ideological education are the three elements essential to women's liberation—that these were the things that made women's equality possible in China and can work as well in the United States.

It is really not so surprising then, that a Federal IWY official at the Colorado IWY conference boasted, "This is the first revolution paid for by the government." Or that in Iowa, an IWY keynote speaker openly contended, "Capitalism must be replaced by the only effective and proven method of government—socialism."[4]

The text of the World Plan answers with striking clarity Mrs. Ulbrich's question, "What will the new emerging trends and policies be?"

"Mr. Chairman," Mrs. Ulbrich went on, "the co-head of the U.S. delegation to Mexico City was Patricia Hutar, a member of the U.S. IWY Commission and president of the National Republican Federated Women's Clubs. The State Department bulletin quotes Mrs. Hutar:

" 'We have a commitment to work together to ensure the full implementation of the Plan of Action in our country. . . .In order to escalate the process of equality for women and for integration in development, we must devise strategies to change attitudes and behavior that have resulted from cultural conditioning. . . .It is the conviction of women globally that the goals of International Women's Year of equality, development and peace are not goals for *women* but serious goals for a world society and that men no less than women stand to gain.' [Emphasis in original.][5]

"Notice, Mr. Chairman, that Mrs. Hutar wants to ensure full implementation of the World Plan as an accomplished fact. She does not speak of any opportunity for the grass roots to modify or even accept it! IWY knows that the effective way to implement a plan in the U.S. is to show grass roots support for the programs. IWY has conjured up synthetic grass roots through the mechanism of the state conferences." She paused, blinking as a photographer's strobe flashed nearby.

Did any congressman or senator listening to this testimony remember that the current presiding officer of the National Commission of the Observance of International Women's Year, Bella Abzug, had not only been the congressional advisor to the U.S. delegation at the UN World Conference on IWY in Mexico City, but had gone home and written the legislation creating Public Law 94-167 that mandated and financed the state women's meetings?

"If there were genuine grass roots support," Jill continued, "the government would not be paying people to try to manufacture that support with five million tax dollars. This manipulation of public attitudes with Federal funds is *not* characteristic of a free society. We are going to reap a wild whirlwind if Congress does not stop the appropriations for IWY activities.

"And, finally, Mr. Chairman, if other countries are planning on the 'new world economic order' being brought into existence through International Women's Year and the International Women's Decade to follow—thereby redistributing the world's wealth—the American people certainly have a right to know exactly what is intended!"

Sisters of the World, Unite

*"It is no accident that the women of Italy...
brought down the Italian government on the
issue of reproductive freedom...We are part
of a worldwide network."* —Gloria Steinem

A distinguished looking gentleman waved his notepad toward the empty aisle seat beside me. "May I sit down and talk with you a few minutes? I'm David Broder of *The Washington Post.*"

"You certainly may." I smiled, welcoming a seasoned professional after the subjective interrogations of feminist reporters saturating the National Women's Conference.

"The ERA battle is going to be the prime test of strength of the women's movement. How will this conference affect its ratification?" Broder asked.

"I'm convinced that IWY activities here this weekend are going to hurt ERA's passage. Both the public and the legislators now understand that ERA proponents are the same people promoting abortion and gay rights. They have seen first-hand that IWY is controlled by radical feminists," I pointed out.

"How did you get involved in this movement?" he probed.

I leaned forward, tapping Patricia Hutar—a member of our Illinois delegation—on the shoulder. "This is the gal who got me started in politics. Remember when you came to Peoria in 1963 speaking for Senator Goldwater?"

Pat nodded. A little more than a decade later, we were diametrically opposed. Sadly, I had watched as she voted not only for ERA, but for the straight feminist Pro-Plan including abortion and gay rights.

Now I could see what Dr. Francis Schaeffer meant when he told us that there is no need for a conspiracy theory:

"To be looking only for the possibility of a clandestine plot opens the way for failing to see a much greater danger: that many of those who are in the most prominent places of influence, and many of those who decide what is news, have the common, humanist world view," he said.

The Houston meeting was, indeed, a "part of a worldwide network." Although the top leadership knew the truth, few delegates realized that they had been sucked into supporting the demise of their own country under the guise of equal rights. They had been programmed to accept the humanistic philosophy without ever realizing it had happened!

Nevertheless, evidence abounded that NWC ties to the international network were inextricably meshed. Identified only by a Post Office Box in France, a broadside, *Women's Movement Plans Actions for an Internationalist March,* outlined goals similar to IWY's National Plan of Action. The handout told of an October meeting in Paris attended by about sixty women from France, Germany, Belgium, Spain, Britain, Switzerland and the United States to "coordinate among themselves on an international level." The initial object of this meeting was to prepare March 8 actions globally, and spelled out an International Manifesto charging Europe, Africa, Asia and America with oppressing women.

"Everywhere in the world the religious powers, the churches, are waging intense ideological campaigns in order to maintain the population under their yoke, thus playing the game of ruling classes," the flyer charged. (Hadn't Karl Marx called religion an opiate of the people?) "We, women of the world, are all in solidarity with each other...we have decided to struggle together in order to impose...the right to free abortion on request, with elimination of laws allowing doctors to refuse to perform abortions for 'reasons of conscience'; the development of sex education; the right to discover our sexuality."

The paper also called for an international tribunal like the UN Commission on Women's Rights to demand the abolishing of laws which make adultery or prostitution a crime.

How many delegates knew that Alexandr Solzhenitsyn, in *The Gulag Archipelago,* identifies March 8 as International Women's Day in communist countries? How many remembered that on March 8, 1975—the official UN International Women's Year—former Congresswoman Bella Abzug, New York's Lt. Gov. Mary Anne Krupsak and Betty Friedan addressed 3,000 persons who marched down Fifth Avenue "expressing solidarity with women around the world"? They carried signs demanding "equal pay for women, universal child care, ratification of ERA, access to abortion, civil rights for lesbians and an end to militarism." According to an AP wire story, they were joined by representatives of left-wing groups! Ms. Krupsak, a NOW member, told the demonstrators: "Women can change the face of the world."

It was Ms. Krupsak—now a member of the IWY Commission—who, with Bella Abzug at her side, chaired the Saturday night session of the National Women's Conference, first "losing" my substitute resolution against ERA, then ruling it defective to prevent a vote.

With my microphone turned off from the platform to preclude any protest, I made my way to the front of the Coliseum. I called up to Ms. Abzug, "Bella, it was such a little thing. You had the delegates to defeat my resolution, but your refusal to allow a vote shows that you have circumvented the intent of Congress to allow all points of view at this meeting."

Surrounded by reporters, she smiled condescendingly from

beneath her broad-brimmed hat. "I had nothing to do with it." She shrugged. "That's parliamentary procedure!"

"If this is equality, then I prefer justice," I told the media through tears. "I'm not crying for myself. I weep for my country."

Within moments, the Equal Rights Amendment was approved without debate, and Karen DeCrow surged past me leading proponents as they chanted, "Three more states, three more states."

There was not a person in the auditorium, including the national press, who did not recognize the heavy-handed tactics of the feminists in power. As David Broder reported, "The one-sided endorsement of ERA late Saturday night triggered the most emotional outburst of the conference. . . .But the one-sidedness of the ERA vote also reflected a political imbalance among the delegates chosen by their state conventions that skewed the tone of the whole convention."

Even IWY Commissioner Congresswoman Margaret Heckler stepped forward to tell me, "I don't agree with your position, but this was handled unfairly."

Jill Ruckelshaus stood by watching indifferently. She had been the first chairperson of the U.S. IWY Commission who, several months earlier, remarked at the National Women's Political Caucus third biennial conclave: "The women's movement in America needs your heart, your soul, your strength. . . .We're going to cut the hearts out of the anti-ERA people."

"Jill," I asked, wiping my eyes with the back of my hand, "why is IWY polarizing women? Why are equal rights only for those of your persuasion? Why would you not even accept inserting the word 'qualified' into the resolution demanding quotas of women appointees to Federal and state policymaking positions?"

"That would be an insult," Ms. Ruckelshaus snapped.

Thus, one Capitol Hill journalist wrote; "I know of nothing I've ever agreed with Betty Friedan on. But when she says of this convention, 'I have never seen anything like this,' I agree. And I hope I never do again. But if I do, I at least hope I'm not helping pay for it."[1]

Yet while Christians watched gavel-to-gavel proceedings of the NWC back home on public TV, how many suspected that the perversion of equal rights in Houston was only the tip of the international Women's Lib iceberg? How many realized that hundreds of the delegates voting for the IWY goals were not "kooks" at all but state legislators and appointed governmental officials who are in a position daily to pass or influence legislation to change the structure of society?

Donated by union printing, the Freedom Socialist Party distributed an "Open Letter to IWY Delegates" headlined, "Women's rights in Peril! Mobilize for Battle!—Right-wing forces across the nation have launched an all-out attack on everything feminists have fought for. . . .The women's movement is at a crossroads. Either we meekly surrender to the reactionary onslaught and perish, or we boldly, candidly engage the enemy. . . .Feminism is now and always has been a radical movement, because our goals and demands are truly revolutionary."

This solidarity of Women's Lib Internationale was confirmed in the fall of 1977 by Audrey Rowe-Colom, national chairperson of the NWPC—the political action arm of NOW (also co-founded by Betty Friedan)—and U.S. IWY Commissioner, when she toured the Peoples' Republic of China.

"Women hold up half the sky. Chairman Mao has declared that women will be equal within our society," Ms. Rowe-Colom reported as being the resounding theme in China. "Many positive institutions evolved such as child care centers all over the place, offering very good care at prices absolutely everybody can afford. . . .China utilizes all of its human resources."[2] (Fully 90 percent of China's women work outside the home.)

Accompanying her was Julia Bloch, former aide to Senator Charles Percy, who is staff director for the Senate Select Committee on Nutrition and Human Needs. She explained that women "with any measure of mobility [in the Peoples' Republic] are those who have a brilliant political ideology."

IWY appears to be operated by the same criteria. In a letter to chairmen of state delegations following the National Women's Conference, Chairperson Abzug invited them to participate in a Committee of the Conference to plan further IWY activities if they agreed to support the National Plan of Action.

Calling from Honolulu, Carmi Richeson exclaimed, "Bella has no intention of being fair, and this letter proves it! Any legislator who votes more money for the IWY farce after this is a fool." (Congress was never asked. On March 22, 1978, President Carter at White House ceremonies commended Ms. Abzug for her "adept handling" of the NWC, and extended the IWY by executive order, and established a new National Advisory Committee for Women* to promote the UN "Equality Development and Peace" Decade for Women and implement the National Plan of Action.[3]

Evidently, only those with a "brilliant political ideology" will be implementing the National Plan and preparing for a second women's conference in 1980!

Women's Lib in Russia is much like China's. The U.S.S.R. has had an equal rights amendment since 1936. Women can get free abortions, paid maternity leave, easy divorce, and when they marry they can keep their maiden names. In addition, virtually all able-bodied women hold full-time jobs.

A writer for *Ms.* magazine was invited to attend the second National Congress of the Federation of Cuban Women, organized after the revolution to increase their involvement in the struggle. She reported that a new maternity law gives all working women four-and-a-half month's leave at full pay, but children can enter the free day-care centers as early as forty-five days. Divorce is easier in the new Cuba, too.

"When I understood that I could work and earn enough money for Lilia [her daughter] and me, that I didn't really need him, and that I could just go to court and explain my situation and have a divorce—well I did it," a Cuban mother told the teacher-turned-reporter. "I'm much happier now."[4]

A proposed Family Code for the island dictatorship would give "complete equality between men and women in marriage, divorce, child support. . ." It is apparently similar to Italy's family law passed in 1975. It had been opposed by the Catholic church because it was likely to undermine family unity. But legal experts hailed the law as another triumph for Women's Liberation. Italian women now are accorded the same rights

115

and duties as men; a man is no longer listed as head of the house, and a woman does not have to acquire the last name of her husband. (The 1980 U.S. Census will eliminate men as heads of households.)

Only the year before, Italy's divorce laws became legal. And in 1976, the Associated Press reported, "Tens of thousands of women marched through downtown Rome waving their clenched fists and shouting slogans against the Pope. . .for his opposition to legalized abortion. It was the biggest feminist rally ever in Italy." In January of that year, women and homosexuals marched in front of the cathedrals of Florence and Turin protesting a Vatican document on sexual ethics supporting historic Christian views.

Not surprisingly, in 1976, the Worldwatch Institute, a research organization, noted that the percentage of the world's population living in countries with liberal abortion laws increased from 38 to 64 percent in five years. One of the prime reasons—growth of the women's movement!

Internationally, Women's Lib has inspired thousands of women in Germany and England to picket, strike and demand their "rights" as well. And one European country attributes the epidemic of head lice on children to lack of attention by liberated mothers.

As Addison observed in the 18th century, "She who does not make her family comfortable will herself never be happy at home, and she who is not happy at home will never be happy anywhere."

The Swedes have proved him correct. For forty years, Sweden's socialist government has provided everything that Women's Lib demands—in return for taxes which run 60 to 70 percent of each family's income. Subsequently, in their last national election, taxpayers threw out the government that had "given" them all these benefits!

In France, Secretary of State for the Condition of Women, Francoise Giroud, has come to an interesting conclusion: "It seems that feminine resignation, which was relatively serene when founded on obedience to the law of God, disappears or turns angry as soon as there remains only the law

Madame Giroud pointed out that a large portion of French women perceive their condition as uncomfortable, meaning unhappy, and that a primary factor of unhappy French women is the decline in church attendance. At least 40 percent of French women have reached the point where they feel marriage is no longer indispensable for the fulfillment of women.

Angry British feminist, Kate Millet, (who showed up at Houston's NWC) insists that "so long as every female, simply by virtue of her anatomy, is obliged, even forced to be the sole or primary caretaker of childhood, she is prevented from being a free human being. The care of children. . .is infinitely better left to the best trained practitioners of both sexes who have chosen it as a vocation, rather than to harried and all too frequently unhappy persons with little time or taste for the work of educating minds however young or beloved. . . . The family, as that term is presently understood, must go."[5]

In her excellent critique of Women's Lib, Arianna Stassino-poulous describes the curious parallel between modern feminists and the pacifists of the 1930s.

"Millett looks at male loyalties and comradeship with her usual mechanical sneer," Miss Stassinopoulous writes. "Regardless of the context in which an army is used and for whatever purpose, she presumably wishes to abolish the military and masculinity together. . . .She develops this theme at great length in an attack on the militarism and male supremacism of Nazi Germany, from which we are expected to conclude that all armies. . .and all male comradeship are evil. . . .Yet who does she think defeated the Nazis?

"Although the threat from Hitler grew, English pacifists vehemently opposed rearmament. . . .But what if the British people's very ability and willingness to fight back had been destroyed by social changes of the kind urged by Women's Lib? Unilateral abolition of masculinity suffers from the same drawbacks as unilateral disarmament. . . .Are we to demand in the true Women's Lib style, 'Women the [life] boats, men and children first. ' "[6]

Other historians have noted the rise of homosexuality within the same time frame as the once-great British Empire moved toward a socialist state.

Not even the Far East has escaped the scourge of feminism. Chupiren, the pink-helmeted women's liberationists of Japan, press for an end to abortion restrictions. In the first issue of *Feminist,* an article attacks Buddhism for subjugating women. Says its female editor, "She [woman] must open her eyes to change, not only in Japan, but in other countries in the world."

Throughout U.S. IWY materials runs the theme that Congress has mandated the Commission to "identify the barriers that prevent women from participating fully and equally in all aspects of national life and develop recommendations for means by which such barriers can be removed."

The most important barrier appears to be worldwide: "The Commission endorses the landmark Supreme Court decision on abortion and asks that other barriers be removed to permit women greater choice with regard to their reproductive lives."

The entire global community has adopted the view that there is no living God; therefore, there are no absolutes, no right or wrong. Call it secular humanism, progressive education, behavioral science, socialism, internationalism, communism, liberalism or feminism—the aim is diabolically synonymous. No wonder Scripture teaches that Satan is the prince of this world. He is, indeed, alive and well on planet earth, urging its sisters to unite!

*The National Advisory Committee for Women includes Bella Abzug, co-chair; Jean O'Leary, Eleanor Smeal and officials of League of Women Voters, Women's Political Caucus, Business & Professional Women's Clubs, American Association of University Women and six labor unions; but NO PRO-FAMILY, PRO-LIFE LEADERS!

"In the Last Days. . ."

"This know also, that in the last days perilous times shall come...evil men and seducers shall become worse and worse, deceiving, and being deceived."—II Timothy 3:1, 13

Perilous times have come. Around the world, St. Paul's predictions to Timothy are everywhere in evidence: men and women are lovers of themselves, covetous, proud, blasphemers, disobedient to parents, unthankful, unholy, without natural affection, trucebreakers, false accusers, despisers of those that are good, traitors, lovers of pleasures more than lovers of God, having a form of godliness, but denying God's power! Christians see the effects in education, government, religion and the women's movement.

No wonder my pastor says, "People are so uptight these days they can't even fall asleep in church!"

One significant sign of the nearness of Christ's second com-

119

ing, according to Bible scholars, is the rise of militant homosexuality. When the disciples asked Jesus what conditions would be like when He returned, He replied, "As it was in the days of Lot." Remember the men of Sodom? They were "without natural affection," demanding perverse sexual relations with angels who came to warn Lot of approaching destruction. So grave was this sin in God's eyes, that throughout all history it has been called sodomy—until our generation invented "alternate lifestyles," "gay rights" and "sexual preference."

Because one woman dared to take a stand against the demands of "gay rights" in Florida and won, Christians tend to believe their community is safe. But they are only kidding themselves.

Shortly after the repeal of the Dade County ordinance, Anita Bryant was scheduled to give a sacred concert in our area. Her appearance had been widely advertised and in the press of IWY activities, I had neglected to order tickets. Less than a week before, I phoned the pastor who had made Anita's arrangements, to ask if there might by chance be a few seats left.

"There are a lot of tickets," he advised me. "They're not selling as we expected."

I was astonished. Where were the believers who claimed to support this courageous woman?

"I'll make some calls," I promised the pastor, "to help generate a crowd. I suppose many like myself thought the concert would be sold out by this time." There were some who had assumed that, but others were afraid of trouble and didn't want to get involved!

In addition, I contacted representatives of Pro-Family organizations and arranged a meeting for us with Miss Bryant to encourage her. When we arrived at the auditorium on Saturday evening, dozens of protestors were outside chanting, "Anita Bryant's gotta go" and "Outta the closets and into the streets." A large banner proclaimed, "Gay Rights are Human Rights," while hand-signs declared, "Homosexuality is not a sin—Discrimination is," "Gay is Good," "Hitler, McCarthy, Bryant," "We *Are* Your Children," "A Day in the Closet is like a Day without Sunshine," and "Squeeze a Fruit for Anita."

While Terry Cosgrove, president of Illinois Men for ERA, told reporters, "She is crudely exploiting religion to serve her own purposes," demonstrators were singing, "Move on over or we'll move on over you. For gay folks, time has come."

"I fought the repeal of the homosexual rights law in Dade County," continued Cosgrove, who had helped plan the IWY Workshop on ERA and had been its official timekeeper! "But I'm pleased that, as a member of the Urbana Human Relations Commission, I helped get a similar human rights ordinance adopted in Champaign!"

God had to raise up a woman in liberal Miami to stand for righteousness, but where had the grass roots ministers, priests and rabbis of Champaign, Illinois, been? Occupied? Jesus' command to us is, "...occupy until I come." The active definition of that verb is "to take hold or possession of, to reside in as an owner or tenant." Yet, when the Illinois House Judiciary Committee considered "gay rights" bills last year, Mrs. Renata Hayes was the only Christian, following a long line of endorsers, to remind legislators, "All nations that become decadent start with condoning homosexuality."

Because of the many threats on Anita Bryant's life, security at the concert was so tight that each of us was required to match his or her Social Security card with the number previously provided. It gave us an uneasy feeling that in America a Christian was being persecuted for her faith.

Backstage, I presented her with a sheaf of roses. "We love you, Anita," I told her, "for standing up for our families. We just want you to know you're not alone in this battle. We're praying for you."

I was surprised, standing next to her behind the drawn curtain, that the lady with such a big voice was so petite. She graciously shook our hands, thanking us for coming. It was hard to understand how her position against homosexuals and lesbians becoming role models for children could have been so misconstrued and maligned in a country whose motto is "In God We Trust."

Where was the national media when IWY Commissioner Jean O'Leary told free-lancer Cindy Miller at the National Gay Leadership Conference in Denver, "After Anita Bryant, the feminists really began defending lesbian rights. The American Civil Liberties Union, National Organization for Women, National Women's Political Caucus, Women's Action League and the League of Women Voters met with the National Gay Task Force to pool our expertise.

"But changing laws is not enough," O'Leary went on. "Our long-range plans are to change attitudes through education. We have a whole program of printed materials geared to churches, unions, teachers, legislators and parents developed by a professional public relations firm in Boston. The priority group now is teachers. We want gay lifestyles integrated into all courses like history and literature."

This, then, is the real implication of the Sexual Preference Resolution passed at the National Women's Conference where any mention of God was shouted down in derision and Ms. O'Leary got a standing ovation! That is why a young woman with a large NOW button gave me a free copy of *A Lesbian Guide* on the floor of the NWC. Although I knew that Chairperson Abzug had introduced a "gay rights" bill as a Congresswoman and that she had instructed state IWYs to include sexual preference workshops, I was appalled to read in bold print on the cover, "This booklet was prepared by the National Gay Task Force and officially approved by the National Commission on the Observance of International Women's Year."

On the first page of *A Lesbian Guide,* under the U.S. Department of State address, was a list of IWY Commissioners purportedly endorsing the contents. Influential names—Liz Carpenter, co-chair ERAmerica; John Mack Carter, *Good Housekeeping* editor; Jane Culbreth, past president of National Federation of Business & Professional Women's Clubs; Claire Randall, general secretary of the National Council of Churches; Gloria Scott, national president of the Girl Scouts; and Senator Charles Percy—gave respectability to the publication. The thrust was revealed in statements like: "Most children were led to believe that every one of their leaders and every other nice person they knew was heterosexual. . . .Lesbians would like children to learn that gay people are not the irresponsible freaks they are supposed to be, but can be warm, strong, sensitive, responsible, *moral* people." [Original emphasis.]

Perpetrating the employment discrimination hoax, the guide states, "There is still considerable resistance to hiring acknowledged lesbians or gay men for any jobs, such as teaching or counseling, involving close contact with young people. The assumption is that homosexuality can be learned, and there is great fear of positive gay role models. It is also thought that gays cannot be trusted with children or young people without 'molesting' them sexually. This is not the view of those in a position to know the facts—for instance, the National Education Association. . ."

Unfortunately, quasi-endorsement of such fiction by prominent Americans does not make it fact. Have the murders of teenaged boys by homosexuals in Texas been forgotten? Or the conviction of two Boy Scout troop masters in New Orleans for preying on their own scouts? Or the exposure of a homosexual minister in the Midwest luring youngsters into his lifestyle? Or the discovery of perverted sex orgies sponsored by the headmaster of an eastern boy's school?

If gays are not encouraging our children to adopt this lifestyle, why did they sell publications—like the sickening hard core pornography *Growing Up Gay* or *What Lesbians Do*—at state and national IWY conferences? Moreover, why did the U.S. government wink at this action sponsored by one of its own commissions? As a policeman told my husband at the Albert Thomas Exhibit Hall in Houston, "Wait 'til I tell my wife what I'm protecting. Ordinarily I'd be raiding a place like this."

Even though Senator Percy wrote me that he did not approve of some things that took place at the NWC, his own IWY Commission obviously knew what exhibits were inside because a sign posted warned, "Some displays may not be suitable for all ages."

This unprincipled mind-set is not peculiar to America. In 1973, the West German Bundesrat passed legislation okaying pornography, group sex, wife-swapping and homosexuality. The Minister of Justice explained that the new law was an attempt to progress from the attitudes and mores of the 19th century.

No doubt the Romans thought they, too, were making progress as the licentious Empire declined. Homosexuality and sex perversions were preceded by a weakening of the father's authority, emancipation of children, women's liberation, avoiding responsibilities of motherhood and childlessness. Commented one historian, "The feminism which triumphed in Imperial times brought more in its train than advantage. . . . By copying men too closely, the Roman woman succeeded more rapidly in emulating man's vices than in acquiring his strength."

Drawing a modern corollary, sociologist Carol Trumpe told an Illinois IWY Showcase audience: "Moral looseness, easy divorce, dissolving of family ties and adultery caused laws against these actions to fall into disuse. The public became sophisticated and ceased to be shocked. Contempt for life was characterized by circuses pitting humans against wild animals. Romans became dependent on big government to provide for them, and they shifted to a volunteer army.

"Criminologists see just such a parallel today. 'Their quest for equal rights has led some women to become vulgar and criminal. . . .It's no coincidence that at the same time women have invaded barrooms and board rooms, four women have made the FBI's Ten Most Wanted list,'" Mrs. Trumpe quoted one authority on crime. "Feminism is a path which history has proved leads to disaster. But we must not forget that the early church requickened the lost and forgotten virtues, temporarily preserving the Empire. Are *we* willing to do the same?"

Another important prophecy appears in two books of the Bible—Daniel and Revelation: a one world government, which is popular today among prominent leaders. The United World Federalists are pushing for an international government through the United Nations. As staff-writer for a local newspaper, I covered a UWF "peace" banquet in 1969.

"The U.S. owes a duty to its own people and to all mankind to advocate the transformation of the UN into a world authority for the control of national power," the speaker—a minister and university professor—said. "The first practical step is the development of a new U.S. foreign policy dedicated to that purpose. We call upon the President to concentrate [on]. . . .

general and complete disarmament. . .under enforceable world law. . .[a] United Nations Peace Force."

UWF goals correspond with positions set forth in Department of State Publication 7277 released in September 1961, entitled, "Freedom from War." They are identical to the views of Women's Lib enumerated at the NWC under the guise of "equal rights!"

No wonder the Veterans of Foreign Wars have passed a resolution[1] opposing world government. It would have direct taxing powers, destroy our sovereignty, confiscate our economic wealth, establish a global currency, strip the U.S. of military independence, and cause everyone to be citizens of the world.

A world president with the unlimited power of a UN peace force at his disposal would be so formidable that all the world might ask, "Who is like the beast? Who is able to make war with him?" (Revelation 13:4.) Who, indeed, with only a handful of civilian policemen for domestic order as IWY's Peace Hearing suggested.

"Let no man deceive you," the apostle Paul warns regarding this antichrist, "for that day shall not come, except there come a falling away [church apostasy] first, and that man of sin be revealed. . .who opposeth and exalteth himself above all that is called God. . .showing himself that he is God. . . .And for this cause God shall send them strong delusion, that they should believe the lie. . ." (II Thessalonians 2:3,4,11).

Dishearteningly, the organized church is fast "falling away" from the faith. Episcopalians have ordained a lesbian into the priesthood in New York. A Methodist minister holds nude therapy sessions in Illinois. In Houston, a Catholic priest with a COYOTE (Call Off Your Tired Ethics—a loose women's organization) button on his clerical robe defended the national prostitute club's rights to have male clients arrested along with hookers at the NWC. ("Had he lost sight of his calling?" Pat Trowbridge, an Illinois observer, wondered.) The Presbyterian Task Force on Homosexuality endorses ordination of gays.

"It's a sad commentary on the church," deplores Dr. Bruce W. Dunn. "We've had people studying the issue two years

125

and they have come up with the wrong conclusion!"

Yet there is not a single passage of Scripture, according to Bible scholars, that condones homosexual conduct as the will of God. As Professor Richard Lovelace reminds Christians, we all fall and are forgiven by seeking God's transforming grace. "This is real Biblical liberation—freedom from the guilt and power of sin. The homosexual does not want to seek this kind of liberation. He simply wants God's stamp of approval on his self-indulgence."

Increased occult activity is another symptom of apostasy. An invitation to a "witches and amazons feminist cultural conference" at the University of Indiana was distributed at the National Women's Conference. It promised a midnight service, with an authority on witchcraft and high priestess of the Susan B. Anthony Coven #1 from the American Academy of Religion as keynote speaker. There is a witches' liberation movement known as WICA—Witches International Craft Association. Burgeoning occult books and movies seem to coincide with ritual murders from the East to the West Coast. Anton LeVey poses as high priest of the First Church of Satan. Similar phenomena are reported spreading in Europe.

Another prophecy that must have seemed strange in Christ's lifetime—considering the Eastern culture—was His prediction, "For, behold, the days are coming in which they shall say, Blessed are the barren, and the wombs that never bare. . ." (Luke 23:29). But even before Women's Lib was full-blown the Population Reference Bureau pronounced, "There are some people who think this may be the last generation with freedom of choice about how many children each family will have."

When presidential hopeful George Bush was a congressman, he headed the Republican Task Force on Population and Earth Resources. "We are trying to assess the resistance to family planning by certain groups. So far, it looks like opposition from religious groups and the black militants isn't too serious."[2] The National Women's Conference proved that!

The Club of Rome—businessmen, economists, and scientists organized around a model world system being developed at

MIT—has even more ambitious plans. Its bible, *The Limits of Growth,* predicts global disaster unless tight controls are imposed on population and every other aspect of society. What kind of government could prescribe the limits on child-bearing and use of resources that the futurist Club of Rome envisions?[3]

One method might be the controversial techniques of behavioral scientists like B.F. Skinner who says, "We need to make vast changes in human behavior." A University of Michigan futurist proposes, "We should reshape our society so that we all would be trained from birth to do what society wants us to do." With the breaking of the DNA code, biological tinkering to modify people before they are born is imminent. The Nazis turned eugenics into a dirty word, using women as breeders for a super race. How much different are modern scientists who benignly assure us that genetic engineering would be used for the betterment of mankind?

In keeping with the prophecy of children being disobedient to parents, the child advocate movement is subtly advancing in that direction. The UN's International Year of the Child in 1979 will promote children's rights!

"I am very concerned about the child emancipation legislation that is being introduced in Illinois," State Representative Mary Lou Sumner told me on the phone. "It is a foot-in-the-door toward taking away parent's rights."

Court rulings overturning state laws requiring parental consent for teenage abortions are obvious cases. Not so noticeable are the student's rights handbooks issued through students councils, and the National Student Lobby. Recent lawsuits have been filed by children against their parents for negligence. And minors are being removed from the custody of parents at the whim of the court. In Milwaukee, a judge ruled that parents did not have the right to treat their daughter's leukemia with laetrile.[4] Perhaps this action is what Gloria Steinem includes in children's rights when she stated at the Nevada IWY, "Children belong to all of us. . ."

The architects of 1984 have not forgotten the ladies. As *The Futurist* magazine advocates, "We thus face the need to demand that the ancient and honorable occupation of motherhood fall into disrepute, and that women commit themselves to other occupations. Women must be 'liberated' to enjoy the fruits of other occupations, *whether they want to be or not.* [Original emphasis.] Unisex will come into fashion. . . .Nothing will distinguish men and women. . .from each other."

Surely the stage may be set for an authoritarian world dictator. And among prophecy students, there always is speculation as to the personality of the beast of Revelation whose number is 666. Now according to Scripture, seven is the perfect number of God and six is the imperfect number of man. Could the rise of humanism, spurred on by international feminism, be the real identity clue—God discarded, man deified?

When God revealed the "last days" to Daniel, the prophet was troubled. "And I heard, but I understood not," he wrote. "Then said I, 'O my Lord, what shall be the end of these things?'

"And God said, 'Go thy way, Daniel; for the words are closed up and sealed till the time of the end'" (Daniel 12:8-9).

Are we living in the days when ancient prophecies are being unsealed? Have we come full-circle from Eden when the serpent beguiled Eve with the lie, "Ye shall be as God"? The price of LIBerty has been grievous from the beginning!

What Can a Christian Do?

"God has a mission for every person; it's your job to find that mission and fulfill it."—
Phyllis Schlafly

"This is Dianne Edmondson from Broken Arrow," the voice on the phone announced. "I'm volunteering to be your Citizens' Review chairman for Oklahoma."

"Great!" I exclaimed. "I'll get a packet of information in the mail to you today."

It was the beginning of a long-distance telephone friendship, and it was Dianne's faith in a prayer-hearing, prayer-answering God that contributed to at least two major miracles for our national Pro-Family coalition in 1977.

More than a dozen state IWY women's meetings already had taken place before Oklahoma's in mid-June, most totally dominated by feminists who passed the core agenda and elected themselves delegates to the National Women's Conference. Only in Ohio and Missouri, where Right To Life organized and joined with the Citizens' Review Committee, did we win a majority of delegates. Ours was not an impressive record.

But because Mrs. Edmondson did not know it couldn't be done, she mobilized Catholics, Baptists, Mormons, Presbyterians, Methodists, Church of Christ members and others to stand up for their beliefs. Oklahoma not only elected an entire slate of Pro-Family delegates, but rejected IWY's prescribed resolutions and passed recommendations that truly reflected the views of Oklahomans. And the libbers walked out!

Syndicated columnist James J. Kilpatrick described the miracle with pithy irreverence: "It takes a considerable time for news to travel eastward from the Indian territories, so it was not until a day or so ago that word reached Washington of a massacre that occurred in Stillwater. . . . What happened, in brief, is that the troops of Bella Abzug got scalped. In a fair fight at the Oklahoma Conference of Women, the women's libbers were out-maneuvered, out-thought, and out-hustled. Ms. Abzug's complacent legionnaires had scheduled a nicely rigged conference, pre-packaged with nicely rigged resolutions, at which a nicely rigged slate of delegates would be elected to the national conference. . .

"Came the dawn and the buses began to roll. Most of the organizing had been done through local churches. By 7 a.m., as Ann Bowker [Dianne's assistant] describes it, 'five hundred good Christian ladies were waiting quietly in line at the Student Union Building of Oklahoma State University.' The libbers were aghast. In the end, the 200 libbers rumped off. . . . The thousand anti-libbers took over the ballroom. That was the final score. . . .Christians 1000; Lions 200!"[1]

By word of mouth, letters and phone, news began to circulate that Oklahoma's success was due to a cassette tape— made by Dianne Edmondson—to inform churches of the attack on the family by humanist/feminists and to motivate women to attend their IWY meeting. She was deluged by orders for her message from every corner of the U.S. In Hawaii, Carmi

Richeson—a businesswoman—used the tape to bring together a coalition of Women for Traditional Values who swept the slate for Pro-Family delegates to Houston! Eddie Myrtle Moore put the cassettes to work in Mississippi where Christians incurred Abzug's wrath by carrying in an American flag for a pledge, having prayer, and even passing a resolution against sin and immorality! Mrs. Moore defused IWY's charges that Mississippi delegates were members of the Ku Klux Klan with signed affadavits affirming none was a Klansman.

Mrs. Edmondson is an example of what one woman with God can accomplish. When she came to Illinois in August to make plans for the NWC, she recounted how she had come to trust the Lord so completely.

"When I was younger, I told Him there were only two things I couldn't bear—my husband leaving me for another woman and a retarded child. God proved me wrong," she said with a laugh. "That is exactly what happened to me. But His grace is sufficient."

Today, Dianne has a wonderful second husband who took a position with an airline just before our Citizens' Review activities began. "The Lord provides everything we need. I wouldn't be here if I didn't have an airfare pass!" she said.

My friend Bobbie Ames is another godly woman who dared to light one candle. Concerned with the trend in public education, she and her husband founded the Perry Christian School in Marion, Alabama. A letter that Mrs. Ames writes to each new high schooler reads:

"Dear Teenager: Did you know that when God created you, He planned a unique personality and a unique life different from every other one of His creations? He endowed you with special talents and abilities and potentials that you could never have dreamed of. He has an exciting plan for your life different from His plan for every other fellow and girl you know. As you discover this plan and pursue it, you may find yourself becoming a leader and decision maker in tomorrow's world. To find God's plan for your life, you will surely find yourself becoming more creative, more concerned for others, and more courageous as you live this Christian life."

I have worked with Bobbie in Eagle Forum whose membership brochure claims the promise of Isaiah 40:21: "They that wait upon the Lord shall renew their strength; they shall mount up with wings as eagles; they shall run, and not be weary; and they shall walk, and not faint." It is not a promise for super spiritual Christians, or wealthy ones, or even for those with known leadership abilities. God meant it for ordinary men and women.

"If you're willing to be a vessel for God to work through, that's all He asks," says Bobbie, who has helped other communities establish Christian education.

You may not be called to start a school, but you could attend board meetings to influence the choice of textbooks or teaching methods. If you are a teacher, you could organize a chapter of the National Educators Fellowship[2] to learn how you can use your moral influence in the classroom. After all, public schools must remain neutral toward religion—not outlaw it.

You may only be an Italian immigrant with a fifth grade education, whose daughter challenges, "If one woman atheist could get prayer out of the schools in the United States, why couldn't one woman with God get it back in?" That's what Rita Warren, author of *Mom, They Won't Let Us Pray,* did for Massachusetts.

Or you might be like the Irish-Catholic school girl who grew up in the South and was familiar with the racial and religious discrimination of a white-hooded mob. After serving overseas in the Army, Nellie Gray went to law school and worked as a civil rights attorney for the U.S. government. Today, Miss Gray is a full-time volunteer devoted to the civil rights of the pre-born, mobilizing thousands of Right to Lifers to the Capitol each January to protest the 1973 Supreme Court abortion ruling.

There is no end to the ways Christians can be the salt—the preservative—of the earth. In "Bing's Last Message,"[3] America's late beloved crooner expressed his concern about the trend of the entertainment business:

"I'm worried now. Pornographic pictures, dirty books and magazines and TV. . . .Moral responsibility is almost indiscernible," Crosby wrote. "Its effect can't be anything but harmful. [Children] see these chic, sophisticated people behaving immorally, salaciously. People living together without benefit of marriage must be the thing to do, they think. . . .I happen to believe that the family is the basis for a sound society. . . .It's my fervent prayer that responsible people. . . will exert their influence in an effort to eliminate this highly objectionable material. . . .When I talked to a TV executive recently and voiced my sentiments, he said to me, 'We're only depicting life as it is.' But I fear that they are depicting life as it is going to be if they are not diverted."

Citizens for Decency Through Law has been working for more than a decade to curb pornography in movies and on newsstands. Pat Cline, secretary of the Normal, Illinois, chapter asked me, "Did you know that the girl on the cover of the January *Penthouse* is 13 years old? This illustrates the point that pornographers will not call a halt without our insistence."

Pat's group has been instrumental in convincing store managers to remove such material from display. Their anti-porn success provoked an anonymous criticism.

"Your campaign to end what you call pornographic material will be defeated by people who do not feel sex is for procreation only," the letter writer complained. "Your narrow-minded ultra-conservative attitudes smack of represssion. There is no law in the U.S. that says you or any person in your questionable group has to buy a copy of any magazine. I'd sign my name but you'd probably picket me." Signed, "A 6th-Grade Teacher."

What have you done to help stop this filth? As St. James (4:17) admonishes: "To him that knoweth to do good, and doeth it not, to him it is sin."

Having small children at home is no excuse. (Ever notice how easy it is to get away to a luncheon or bowling?) The national PTA television commission needs monitors to help report the increasing violence on TV. According to Dr. Joyce Sullivan, of the home and family life department at Florida State University, the average child sees 13,000 killings on television between the ages of 5 and 15. The PTA notes that this violence contributes to aggressive behavior among youth.

Some will be incited to commit violent acts in direct imitation of those seen on TV. In Lincoln, Illinois, that truth was brought home with bloodcurdling horror when a young man viewed the teleplay of the Manson family, then went out and slaughtered a farm family.

Irene Conlan, wife of former Congressman John Conlan, shares how women can become aware of and active in decision-making processes. "By and large, Christian women seem to be a fairly complacent group," she says. "The attitude is, 'I need to be home with my family,' which is a number one priority. But that doesn't mean women are not supposed to make a contribution to society at the same time. . .

"Legislators count one letter or phone call as representing 100 other people who might have called or written. If just one Christian woman gets ten of her friends to write a letter, that amounts to ten letters, each representing 100 letters or calls. I see so many things women can do without getting their priorities mixed up. When godly women start having an impact on other women and on some of the problems in the community and the country, things will begin to improve."[4]

An early chaplain of the U.S. Senate, Edward Everett Hale, once said: "I am only one, but I am one. I cannot do everything, but I can do something. What I can do, I should do. And what I should do, by the grace of God I will do."

Is that your prayer? Be careful! Several years ago, author Pat Brooks prayed, "Lord, if You want me fighting the avalanche of evil in our nation, I'm available. I'll do whatever You want." Not long afterward, she learned that was a dangerous prayer! "God has a way of taking us at our word, just as He wants us to take Him at His word," she says. Mrs. Brooks became a leader in New York's Operation Wake-Up which defeated a state referendum on ERA by a whopping 400,000 votes.

Yes, Christian women are beginning to make an impact on society. And it is the anti-family, anti-God crowd that is noticing. *Ms.* magazine's cover story for September 19, 1977, concluded; "All feminists have a stake in the gay rights struggle. . . . People who make a noise about homosexual marriage as a consequence of the ERA are going to be uncomfortable about a lot of the things that radical feminism stands for. And whether we like it or not, the issues of feminism and gay rights have now been linked by our enemies if not by ourselves. Feminists of whatever sexual preference can expect to see much more of Anita Bryant. Her allies in the newly solidified national 'antipermissiveness' right wing include Schlafly, with whom she marched against the ERA, Marabel Morgan, and the leaders of the anti-abortion movement....And they're winning."

A fund-raiser mailing on *The Humanist* letterhead in April 1977 complained, "The humanist values we hold dear are under attack—the strongest attack in years. Who'd have thought. . .that a bill (the so-called Conlan Amendment) to prohibit Federal funds for any educational program involving 'secular humanism' would have been only narrowly defeated in the Congress of the United States....Or that humanist textbooks would be censored, as in West Virginia. Or that (shades of the Scopes trial!) fundamentalists would once again demand that evolution no longer be taught to children. Yet all of this has happened in recent months. And more is on the way—organized, led, and financed by the familiar forces of the evangelical right."

It was late Friday afternoon in February 1976. I was, as Erma Bombeck puts it, "shoveling out the cave." Between trips to the state capitol 70 miles away to lobby against ERA, and speaking engagements across the state, my housekeeping had totaled zero! As I poked my dustmop under a bed, the telephone rang—again.

"This is Phil Donahue. I wonder if you and some of your Eagle Forum members would be available to do a talk show with Dr. Harris Rubin on WGN-TV Monday morning?"

I hesitated. Friends were always kidding me about being on television—especially since I had kicked off Eagle Forum's protest of Rubin's "sex-pot" experiment at a state university with several press conferences the previous month.

"I'm not sure."

"We have invited Dr. Rubin to go on at 11 o'clock. I'd like to set aside a block of seats up front for you to discuss your opposition to his project."

"Well, it's pretty late notice, but I'll do my best to get a crowd."

I made several calls to get the trip in motion, but I prayed, "Lord, I don't want to go. Not after reading the grant application for Federal funds. How can anyone talk about Dr. Rubin's obscene procedure on the air? Please send a snowstorm so I won't have to go!"

And He answered my prayer as He always does. Monday morning was cloudy, but the roads were perfectly clear as six reluctant, yet obedient women—a Mennonite, a Catholic, a Methodist and three Presbyterians—started the three-hour trip to Chicago. God had said, "Go. Be witnesses for Me on network TV."

Although Dr. Rubin's explanation of his experiment—to show pornographic films to males inhaling marijuana smoke with devices attached to their bodies to measure erotic reaction—was shocking, neither he nor Donahue embarrassed anyone in our party personally. I did have the opportunity to explain that the project was actually illegal since a controlled substance was to be used. (The Federal District Attorney had threatened to file charges if the professor continued with his plan. Eagle Forum had sent many wires and letters to the U.S. Attorney General asking him not to approve the use of an illegal drug, and to the Secretary of HEW asking him to withhold Federal tax money for such an immoral, unnecessary program having no medical benefits.)

"Well, I'm going to get the money anyway," he smirked.

But later that spring, Congress withdrew appropriations for the "sex-pot" study. The flood of correspondence from Christians had prompted lawmakers to scrap the $120,000 offensive boondoggle!

Why was that experiment approved in the first place? Dr. Francis Schaeffer explains, by tracing the rise and decline of Western Christian culture, how the world view has become warped. Until the middle of this century, our art, music, literature, morals and public laws were based on Biblical principles, he says. But with the escalation of situation ethics and God-is-dead theologians, Christian influence in all areas of society begins a dramatic drift. Absolutes, right and wrong, are considered old-fashioned. A breakdown of laws, government and families creates chaos, and out of chaos, historically, an authoritarian rule—whether by one man or an elite few—emerges.

"How can Christians read the newspapers," asks Schaeffer, "and not understand what is happening? Out of chaos, as humanistic pressures mount prior to Christ's return, we have two choices: an imposed authoritarian order or a revival of Christian truth which gives unity to all knowledge of life."

Shall we be satisfied with the feminists' "new world economic order" imposed on us, content in our "evangelical ghetto," as Schaeffer so aptly describes the lack of Christian involvement? If we remain apathetic, we are surely disobeying our Lord's command to "occupy until I come."

God does not need a majority to accomplish His purposes. If we are willing to deny ourselves, as did Jesus Christ, "Who, being in the form of God, thought it not robbery to be equal with God: But made himself of no reputation, and took upon him the form of a servant. . ." (Philippians 2:3)), we can turn the tide.

With God, All Things Are Possible

"To Thee we raise thankful hearts for deliverance from forces of evil...Awake us each time to a sense of our responsibility in saving the world from ruin."—George Washington's prayer at Valley Forge.

Many of us were "doubting Thomases," to say the least. "If we couldn't get Christian women out to many of the state IWY meetings, how will they ever go all the way to Texas?" some of us wondered. "And the weekend before Thanksgiving, too!"

But a Bible teacher from Fort Worth put on the full armor of God (Ephesians 6:11-18) and met the challenge of Women's Lib head-on. Lottie Beth Hobbs was proposing a National Pro-Family Rally to coincide with the National Women's Conference in Houston.

"You realize that the burden will fall on your women in Texas," Phyllis Schlafly cautioned.

"I can make another tape for churches," Dianne Edmondson offered. "How about calling it, 'Where Do We Go from Here?' and suggest they charter buses to the rally?"

I called Cincinnati's Right to Life executive secretary, Stephanie Varga. "If we can get thousands to march in Washington, we can get them to Houston, too," Miss Varga thought. And Right to Lifer Doris Wilson was certain her group could charter a plane from Utah.

Miss Hobbs agreed to shoulder the responsibility for locating a place to hold the rally, arranging the program, and supervising the million details required for an event of such magnitude. Mrs. Edmondson cut the tape, and I sent out an announcement to my Citizens' Review mailing list of 50. Another miracle was in the making.

The demand for Dianne's "Where Do We Go from Here?" was beyond anyone's wildest imagination. While orders for her first tape reached several thousand, requests for the new cassette more than doubled that! A network of like-minded women was meshing from coast to coast.

In Houston, Life Advocates, Association of the W's, Right to Life, Eagle Forum, Relief Society and other organizations offered to help with the rally. Suzanne Thomas handled publicity. Together with Nellie Gray, Lottie Beth prepared four Pro-Family Resolutions that could be signed by those unable to attend who wanted to vote against IWY's National Plan of Action. A housewife volunteered to receive and count the incoming resolutions. Reproduced by the thousands around the nation, our *Request to the President and to Congress* read:

SINCE HISTORY CONFIRMS THAT THE FAMILY IS THE FOUNDATION OF ALL STABLE SOCIETIES: AND SINCE YOU, AS OUR ELECTED OFFICIALS, HAVE THE RESPONSIBILITY OF MAKING DECISIONS WHICH DIRECTLY AFFECT THE FAMILIES OF THIS NATION, BOTH NOW AND IN THE FUTURE,

I, A CITIZEN OF THE UNITED STATES, SUBMIT THE FOLLOWING RESOLUTIONS TO YOU, WITH DEEP CONCERN, AND WITH AN URGENT REQUEST THAT ALL LEGISLATION BE ENACTED ACCORDING

TO THESE INHERENT PRINCIPLES.

****

WHEREAS each human being from conception through-out the natural continuum of life has value and dignity before the law, and the killing of innocent human beings is an anathema to our society, and

WHEREAS a mother and her pre-born child have an equal right to live, and all reasonable efforts and ordinary means should be used to save the lives of either or both persons when endangered,

THEREFORE BE IT RESOLVED that the Congress enact and the States ratify a mandatory Human Life Amendment to the Constitution to protect all persons born and pre-born from conception.

****

WHEREAS child-rearing is the God-given responsibility and privilege of parents, not the government, and

WHEREAS Federally-controlled Early Child Develop-ment Programs empower the government to choose the ideology by which young lives are molded,

THEREFORE BE IT RESOLVED that pre-school child development programs shall be controlled by the private sector, giving parents freedom of choice over the physical and philosophical environment of their children.

****

WHEREAS existing Federal laws guarantee equality of opportunity in important areas such as employment, ed-ucation, and credit, and

WHEREAS a strict constitutional rule requiring equality between the sexes at all times does not respect the dif-ference between men and women in their child-bearing function and their physical strength, and

WHEREAS the proposed Equal Rights Amendment would transfer enormous new powers from the States to the Federal government,

BE IT RESOLVED that we oppose the ratifica-tion of the Equal Rights Amendment to the Constitution.

****

WHEREAS all personal individual rights are protected by the Constitution, and

WHEREAS the traditional family has proven to be beneficial to society,

THEREFORE BE IT RESOLVED that homosexuality, lesbianism, or prostitution shall not be taught, glorified, or otherwise promoted as acceptable through the laws of society, through the adoption of children, or within institutions such as our schools.

(note: you may strike out any portion of these resolutions with which you disagree)

NAME _____

ADDRESS _____

CITY/STATE/ZIP _____

_____

Send resolutions to:
PRO-FAMILY, PRO-LIFE COALITION
P.O. Box 38609
Houston, Texas 77088

(They will be sent to Washington. It would be very helpful if you can also send a donation - ANY SIZE! You may send for additional copies of this leaflet, or duplicate it, for extensive distribution).

(Each person should sign a separate RESOLUTION page)

By now, IWY officials had gotten wind of our plans, and they tied up every hotel ballroom and meeting hall large enough to accommodate our rally. The Texas women were undaunted. They kept searching for a location and praying!

In mid-October, Lottie Beth wrote me: "The momentum building in various parts of the nation is incredible, encouraging and thrilling. Valiant workers in Tennessee say they have chartered 50 buses. Planes and buses are scheduled from Alabama, Georgia, Louisiana, Kansas, Missouri, Utah,

California, Mississippi—to name just a few. At least one group is driving all the way from New York! More than 25 busloads are coming from the Fort Worth area. The Houston and South Texas people are working very hard. I've just returned from there. To see all the mail pouring in—resolutions from every state—is one of the most amazing and thrilling sights you can imagine!"

Her enthusiasm was contagious. Still there was no place to hold the rally. She had taken a bold step of faith, and never doubted that the Lord would provide.

The three weeks prior to the conference went by in a blur of speechmaking, late-night strategy phone calls, and preparing my testimony for Congressman Robert Dornan's (R.-Calif.) ad hoc congressional hearing which he was taking to Houston on November 19. The national media received from Elaine Donnelly, Citizens' Review media chairman, carefully documented press packets backgrounding our Pro-Family coalition and swamped us all with hours of long-distance interviews. Even *U.S. News and World Report* called to send a photographer to "shoot" me in my kitchen for their National Women's Conference coverage, "Why Women's Lib is in Trouble."[1]

"I think this is a feminist plot to make me clean up the kitchen," I kidded the newsman.

Kathy Teague, Citizens' Review advisory board member and public relations professional, flew to Houston to set up a press room for our coalition. She persuaded the downtown Ramada Inn to alter their commitments to accommodate us.

My phone rang constantly with reports like the one from New Mexico. "I've circulated 10,000 resolutions in the southern half of our state," Maude Rathgeber announced, "and we're lining-up people for the rally."

There was bad news, too. "Did you hear about Ann Kitzmiller's accident?" Stephanie Varga asked.

"Oh, no," I responded. Ann was our key Eagle Forum organizer in Ohio.

"She fell asleep at the wheel returning from a speaking engagement."

Ann was hospitalized and would not be able to serve as a delegate to the NWC, but she was not seriously injured.

And then the call I had been waiting for came. A Christian businessman had secured the Astro-Arena in the Astro-Dome Complex for our rally. It seated 12,000.

"Oh, Lottie Beth, can we fill it? And how will we pay for it?"

"Enough contributions have come in with the resolutions to make a down payment," she said. "And we'll pass the hat at the rally."

The banquet room at the Ramada was jammed with Pro-Family delegates, some who had brought their husbands along, and rally-goers who had arrived early. As we filed past the informal buffet table, I realized that neither Miss Hobbs nor Senator Gubbins, who was to be our Pro-Family floor leader, had arrived. So I did what seemed proper. Leaving my place in line, I clapped for attention.

"Before we begin," I called out, "shall we take a minute to pray? Heavenly Father, thank You for the opportunity to be here on this historic occasion. We know that each of us is here by Your grand design, to be Your ambassadors this weekend. Thank You for the freedom we have, yet, in this land to meet together in Your name. We pray for the rally tomorrow, and for Senator Gubbins—that You will give her the wisdom she needs to direct us. And now we ask Your blessing on this food, that it will strengthen our bodies so we may better serve You. We just thank You and praise You, in the name of our living Lord. Amen."

After dinner, Lottie Beth introduced rally speakers who already had arrived. Mildred Jefferson, Boston physician who serves as national Right to Life president, got a standing ovation. Nellie Gray spoke. Elaine and I were presented from the Citizens' Review Committee. Joan Gubbins closed by reading the account of Gideon (Judges 7). The similarity between his 300 soldiers and our Pro-Family delegates was remarkable. We stood for a final prayer, then Ann McGraw again led us in "God Bless America" as TV cameras rolled and journalist's strobes flashed. It was a spiritual encounter. With denominational ties stripped away, we were united in

Christ. We had done all that was humanly possible without funds or formal organization. Now the "battle was the Lord's"!

To say that the opening of the National Women's Conference was depressing is an understatement. Because there were nearly as many credentialed press as delegates on the floor, a big production was made of carrying in an American flag with the torch that had been brought by runners from Seneca Falls, New York (site of the first National Women's Party Meeting) to the Sam Houston Coliseum. But not even the media's watchful eye persuaded IWY officials to allow an invocation. All Chairperson Abzug permitted was a moment of silence!

A parade of celebrities and first ladies—Ladybird Johnson, Betty Ford and Rosalynn Carter—praised the meeting and plugged the Equal Rights Amendment. We wondered if they had read the National Plan of Action they were endorsing.

"I can't wait until 1 o'clock when the rally begins," Dianne Edmondson whispered as we stood vainly in line for a microphone. "I know I'll feel better then," she said, adjusting her gold "majority" ribbon designed by Right to Life for identifying Pro-Family delegates.

In the crush of parliamentary maneuvering, as voting on the Plan of Action got underway, I lost track of time. Around 3:30 that afternoon, reports began to trickle back from the Astro Arena: 8,000. . .12,000. . .15,000 in attendance!

"Why didn't you people have a phonebank there?" one newsman asked me. "There was only one pay telephone in the whole place to file our stories."

"I guess we never thought of it. . .or had the money to do it," I replied. "Thanks for covering the rally, though!"

The Lord had pulled off an undeniable miracle—with a little help from Christian women. Inside the Coliseum were nearly 2,000 IWY delegates who had come because the Federal government paid their way. But across town more than seven times as many Americans with old-fashioned beliefs about God, home, and country had paid their own way to stand up for traditional moral values! Now we knew the answer to the

Psalmist's question, "If the foundations be destroyed, what can the righteous do?" (Psalm 11:3.) Persevering in the face of insurmountable odds, we had fulfilled Jesus' command, "Let your light so shine before men, that they may see your good works, and glorify your Father which is in heaven" (Matthew 5:16).

"As the cab turned into the Astro-Complex, I had a strange feeling of apprehension," Elaine Donnelly told Jim and me at breakfast the next morning. "It was such a tremendous risk, and I knew the national press would focus on empty seats as evidence that the Pro-Family Coalition couldn't compete with Women's Lib. A big stadium ahead of us was almost deserted. My heart sank!

"Then the driver turned a corner into the parking lot. Row after row after row of buses were neatly lined up from dozens of states. A huge crowd was streaming toward the Arena from cars, campers and vans. Entire families with homespun signs, fathers carrying children piggyback, waved and blew kisses to friends. The happiest thing I heard as I picked my way through the crowded aisles to reach the front," Elaine said, "was that there were no more seats! People were hugging each other, tears in their eyes. No one could believe the rally was such a thundering success.

"Reporters and television network correspondents were everywhere with microphones, cameras and surprised expressions." She giggled. "I found a chair at the back of the stage. I could see state delegation signs bobbing all over the floor and in the upper tiers. Some of them read, 'God is a Family Man,' 'We're Ladies, Not Libbers,' 'Sin is still Sin, Even if its Legal,' and 'IWY means Immoral Women's Year.' A pretty young girl in blue jeans and fashionably frizzy hair carried an American flag and a bright red sign, 'America—You're Paying for the $5 Million Feminist Festival.' (She was featured in *Time* coverage.)

"I was deeply moved by the spectacular panorama before me. Children's choirs, working men, mothers, and young people of all races, religions, occupations and nationalities joined in spiritual and patriotic songs. Several thousand who were turned away by the fire marshal patiently listened from outside. File boxes of Pro-Family resolutions were stacked six feet high all around the platform. I could see columnist James J. Kilpatrick perched cross-legged on the side of the stage behind a stack of resolutions, while Washington writer Barbara Howar—darling of the Jet Set—sat stiffly in the front row looking stunned!" Elaine exclaimed, pausing for breath.

"Oh, how I wish we could have been there," I lamented, pouring a cup of coffee for Senator Gubbins who had joined us.

"How did the speakers go over?" Joan asked.

"They were terrific," Elaine said, giving us a rundown of the program.

Dr. Jefferson, the first black woman graduated from Harvard Medical School, told the rally: "We cannot accept the idea that women who think that they have been oppressed should become oppressors at the first opportunity. The pro-abortion culture has seized control of the IWY conference."

"God is on our side," Phyllis Schlafly emphasized. "We have somebody on our side who is more powerful than the president of the United States."

Blasting Women's Lib and the NWC only five miles away, black Legislator Clay Smothers exhorted, "I have had enough civil rights to choke a hungry goat. I ask for public rights. President Carter says the minority vote put him in office. Well, he's wrong," Smothers disputed. "It was the Christian vote! Join us today, Mr. Carter. Let's do something about those misfits and perverts over in the Sam Houston Coliseum. I want to segregate my family from them." He brought the crowd to its feet with, "I'm sick and tired of the presidents' wives flim-flamming with these libbers!"

Former Green Beret Robert Cramer spoke against the awful reality of women being drafted and serving in combat under ERA. "I don't want my wife and daughter to face what I lived through in Vietnam. Wars are won on battlefields with bayonets and grenades and that's no place for a lady!"

Anita Bryant sent a filmed word of encouragement: "If God be for us, who can be against us."

"ERA is another insidious attempt to erase distinctions. Rejecting the authority of God when He created two sexes isn't liberation but a bitter bondage," said author Elizabeth

Elliott whose missionary husband, Jim, was murdered by Aucca Indians in South America. "The sexes are not interchangeable and we cannot permit women to be judged by the same criteria as men. The difference in sexes' preserves the family. Christ came to make us free. For the Christian woman, submission is not weakness, femininity is not frivolity. Let me be a woman!"

With the fiery rhetoric of a Patrick Henry, Congressman Dornan told of observing the NWC earlier in the day. "Mrs. Lyndon Johnson, Mrs. Gerald Ford, and First Lady Rosalynn Carter were sitting together on the platform—by their presence at Bella Abzug's side giving approval to sexual perversion and the murdering of babies in their mother's wombs."

The audience roared when Dornan invited them to "tell the President his wife went to the wrong rally!"

"How can President Carter ignore us?" Elaine asked. "How can he turn his back on all these Pro-Family people? Many of them voted for him because of his professed moral values."

"How many Pro-Family resolutions did we get?" I questioned.

"Oh, yes, you should have heard the cheers when Lottie Beth announced 300,000 and still counting!" (More than 500,000 finally were delivered to Congress—far more than the Pro-Plan votes that passed the National Plan of Action.)

The success of the rally boosted our sagging spirits. It gave Pro-Family delegates the will and courage to stick it out. By Monday afternoon, our registered parliamentarian, Joan Blankenship, had a headache from futilely protesting IWY's infractions of their own rules—to say nothing of Roberts Rules of Order. A delegate from Oklahoma, Mrs. Blankenship summed up the NWC:

"To put it mildly, the conference was a disaster in parliamentary procedure. There were some periods where total chaos reigned. When the Women's Department issue came up, no one was sure what was finally adopted. As the chair said, 'I will reread. . .because you're not able to hear and vote correctly.' So we voted about three times until it was to *her* satisfaction!"

If, as Scripture says, "the testing of your faith worketh patience" then there must be several hundred women with at least 100 percent more patience! Although much of the press had expected physical confrontation because of the misleading information distributed by IWY, they were disappointed.

"We are going to be ladies at all times," I told Houston Bureau Chief Nick Chriss who covered Pro-Family activities for the *Los Angeles Times.* "If there are any disruptions, they will not be caused by our delegates."

For four days we had been verbally harrassed, shoved from microphones, and consistently out-voted. Our victory was in preventing IWY from claiming unanimous support of their humanist/feminist resolutions. And the nation had watched the unadulterated spectacle of Women's Lib.

A British newsman commented, "I have never interviewed so many angry women who wish a country to be like Russia... such unlady-like behavior. I must step lightly with interviews because these women truly hate men."

By the "unchangeable" rules in the *Federal Register,* it was past time for the conference to adjourn but the program dragged on. Circulating on the floor, I met Senator Gubbins waiting at a microphone.

"I have permission from IWY's parliamentarians to submit our minority report," she said, holding up an officially signed statement. "Wait right here. If they won't let me present it, we're going to walk out. Our delegates are going to miss their planes if this goes on much longer."

The facilitator waved a colored card in front of the microphone. Finally, the Chair recognized Joan—then ruled her out of order!

I made a hurried sweep of one side of the convention floor. "We're walking," I alerted Pro-Family delegates. "Let's go!"

Joan brought delegates from her side of the floor, the media in hot pursuit. Someone began "God Bless America." Behind us, Pro-Plan delegates chanted," ERA, ERA!"

"Why are you walking out, Senator?" a newsman shouted.

"I'm not going to have these delegates miss their flights. With the Thanksgiving holiday, they may not get another. We have done what our constituents elected us to do—vote against this IWY farce."

We were pushed along toward the official IWY press room. Reporters kept asking questions before the senator could get to the podium. I took her briefcase and laid our coats on a table.

"What do you think the impact of this conference will be?"

"What is the story on a threat to one of your delegates?"

"Why do you say this meeting was rigged?"

"Wa-ait a minute!" Senator Gubbins smiled throwing up her hands. "One at a time. The impact IWY wanted was to propagandize their viewpoint and present it as the view of the majority. Presiding Officer Abzug said in her opening remarks, 'Sun of freedom shine in on our deliberations. . .and let democracy be what it should be.' Then Ms. Abzug and the National Commission proceeded to pull down the shade to obliterate the 'sun of freedom' and prove to the American people that they believe what 'democracy' should be is a feminist dictatorship! What they now show is that they are for issues most Americans disagree with."

"Why was a delegate threatened?"

"There was a group in the gallery with a terrorist name on their T-shirts. They took telephoto pictures of us all weekend. At one point, they told a black Pro-Family delegate from Indiana they were going to 'cut her up.' She was terrified. They were waiting for her when we left that night, but some of the ladies' husbands escorted her to the hotel. It just proves that feminists cannot tolerate any viewpoint but their own. Our black delegate from Mississippi resigned because of similar threats."

"You said at an earlier press conference this meeting was rigged. Can you explain?"

"Be happy to," she answered. "I was advised of the feminists' strategy to have the Chair recognize only Pro-Plan caucus delegates in order to cut off debate. This was done resolution after resolution. Microphones were so situated that feminists could line up and keep us from getting to one. Points of parliamentary procedure, which take precedent, often were not recognized by the chair. Ms. Abzug was seated beside the rostrum giving and receiving signals in order to by-pass our people. Points of order, that are always in order and take precedent, were ignored or ruled out of order. This confer- ference was ruthlessly rigged to stifle free speech, assure the expression of only the extremist, feminist philosophy and passage of only the 'approved' resolutions."

"Why do you oppose the National Plan of Action, Senator Gubbins?"

"Well, it would cost many billions of dollars, immensely increase the Federal bureaucracy and intervention into the lives of freedom-loving Americans. The resolutions demand homosexuals have the right to marry, adopt children, and teach in schools. . .they take away the right to life of the unborn. . . they create a unisex society and mandate the Federal government as a cradle to grave 'sugar daddy.' "

At that moment, with the press still asking questions, Bella Abzug came through the swinging doors with her entourage of IWY commissioners. Only the Lord had known when the conference was going to adjourn, and He had given us perfect timing. In the final moments of that unforgettable weekend, Christians had upstaged Women's Lib!

"Hello, Bella." Joan grinned, promptly stepping down.

"I hope we'll meet again sometime," Ms. Abzug said, her hatbrim bobbing as she nodded her head.

"I'm sure we will," the senator replied, throwing the reporters a farewell wave.

"What are you going to do now?" pressed a newsman near her.

She paused for a split-second, then flashed him a tired smile. "I'm going home to put a turkey in the oven for my family!"

Only the Beginning

"The world has never had a good definition of the word liberty, and the American people, just now are much in want of one."—Abraham Lincoln

The National Women's Conference is over, but the battle cry of Women's Lib is only beginning! Claiming a spirit and a unity of historic proportions, IWY leaders sent thousands of followers home on a phony mission to "end discrimination once and for all."

In her "Briefing from the Top," President Carter's assistant, Midge Costanza, told conferees, "You are going to defeat those elected officials who do not support our sensitivities. Anyone who doesn't think the past four days were committed to political action is crazy. . ."

The day after I returned home from Houston, Jacqueline Thomas, who had covered the NWC for the *Chicago Sun*

151

Times, called to interview me for a wrap-up feature. "What do you think the upshot of the conference will be?"

"We have made our point to Congress that feminists do not speak for all American women. The conference proved conclusively that the people behind ERA also are supporting abortion, gay rights and legislation that would restructure our society," I reiterated.

"Pro-Plan delegates say Houston was a turning point in the women's movement; that they now have their act together. Would you agree?" Ms. Thomas queried.

"Well, you know what the Bible says. . .'all things work together for good to them who love God.' Perhaps the five million dollars spent on IWY was the best thing that ever happened." I laughed wryly. "The silent majority has been awakened. In the past, women of traditional moral values have been content to pursue our careers, care for our families and do volunteer work. IWY has demonstrated that the feminist movement has some pretty radical aims. Our Pro-Family women now know who we are and where we are. I think you'll be seeing more real grass-roots input into the political process."

Appropriately, her story was titled, "For Women, No Turning Back After Houston." For sure, the feminists will not. As one national IWY commissioner—a divorcee—told Ms. Thomas, "I took a vow of poverty to do this."

That is costly devotion to a cause. Are Christians even half that committed to their values? The Scriptures do not mince words: "He who is not with Me [Christ] is against Me." The modern adage puts it another way, "If you are not a part of the solution, you are part of the problem!"

So, you say, if all these unpleasant things are going to happen in the end times anyway, why should I bother? God answers, "Resist the devil" (James 4:7). And He exhorts, "Be vigilant, because your adversary, the devil, like a roaring lion walketh about, seeking whom he may devour; whom resist steadfast in the faith" (I Peter 5:8-9).

Both the Bible and secular history attest that humanism's theory is a fraud. It is the lie of the ages. Society does not get better and better by man's way. It always has been at its best when God's laws have been honored. But before 1977 was over, Bella Abzug had sent delegates a letter, urging us to help implement the National Plan of Action.

"Dear Delegate," it read. "On behalf of the members of the National Commission, I want to thank you for making the National Women's Conference an outstanding achievement. Your serious and thoughtful participation, your disciplined behavior and your enthusiasm and spirit all contributed to the success of an event that has captured the imagination of our nation."

Did she really attend the same meeting, I wondered.

"In one of many favorable press reports on our Conference," the letter continued, *"Time* magazine. . .commented: 'What happened, particularly for the 14,000 who attended the Houston meeting, was an end to the psychological isolation that had constrained their activities and ambitions. They learned that many other middle-of-the-road, American-as-Mom's apple-pie women shared with them a sense of second-class citizenship and a craving for greater social and economic equality. . .'

"Now we must put that excitement to work to help accomplish the goals of our National Plan of Action. . . .Here are some suggestions on what you can do to help make the Plan a reality:

"Write to your local papers. . .to the president and to your representatives in the House and Senate thanking them for having made our Conference possible. . .send a group to meet with your national and state legislators to report to them directly on the Conference and our National Plan. . .speak about the National Plan to individuals and organizations in your community to help them become familiar with the objectives. . ."

"You can bet Pro-Family women will speak out," I told myself. "But it won't be the way Ms. Abzug wishes."

The front lines have been drawn, and it is truly a No *Man's* Land! The storm troops of Women's Lib are entrenched in governmental outposts, one hand reaching into the public purse, the other upstretched in a sisterly clenched fist salute. Corrie ten Boom's wisdom, learned in a Nazi concentration camp because Christians once closed their eyes to reality, bears repeating: "A part of God's strategy is to appoint the place where we have to fight. We cannot escape the war by looking for another front line."

On Sunday morning we sing "Onward Christian soldiers, marching as to war." But do we really mean it? We can stem the current engulfing our families, our churches and our nation. If every believer wrote only eight letters—to the local newspaper, President Carter, state and Federal representatives—expressing opposition to the objectives of the Plan of Action, there would be no question who the majority is! So far, lawmakers have heard only the increasingly strident voices of Women's Lib.

Not only are feminists in control of IWY, but they are everywhere in dominant positions. On January 19, 1978, IWY commissioner Anne Saunier, who received national recognition for chairing Sunday's National Women's Conference, became a member of the advisory committee on the rights and responsibilities of women at the U.S. Department of Health, Education and Welfare. A member of NOW's national board, she said, "The purpose of the committee will be to advise Secretary Califano. Because the budget is so large and the programs so diverse and almost every program they have affects women, it's a real opportunity to affect the policies and programs of HEW."[1]

The advisory committee will be chaired by Eileen Hernandez, a past president of NOW. If IWY was an advisory committee to the State Department, what bitter fruits will HEW's new advisory committee bear? Since HEW already has abolished boys' choirs and nearly made mother-daughter/father-son banquets illegal, what advice will this new group give Califano?

These are the caliber of women which the NWC voted to policy-making positions on an equal basis with men. When I wrote to President Carter asking why he named Jean O'Leary, a lesbian, to the IWY and had not selected any evangelical born again Christian whom he claims to represent, I received a reply from Midge Costanza:

"In March of this year, the National Gay Task Force requested that I meet with their representatives in order to give gay people an opportunity to outline their grievances with the Federal government. I accepted that invitation in keeping with the President's commitment that access be given to all groups. . .

"I will never apologize for providing any groups with the opportunity to participate in their government."

"Great," I said to myself. "She didn't answer my question to the President but I'll take her up on meeting with Pro-Family women."

"What group is it that wants to meet with Ms. Costanza?" her aide asked when I dialed the White House.

"Pro-Family, Pro-Life women who have been shut out of IWY planning and policy-making decisions," I answered.

"Oh, them!"

"You mean, gays have a right to the opportunity but Pro-Lifers do not?"

"I'm not going to answer that question."

I paused. "Are you a born again Christian like the President?"

"A what?" she shouted in my ear.

"A Christian. . .like President Carter."

"No!" she snapped.

So much for equal rights at 1600 Pennsylvania Avenue.

Feminist philosophy also is faring well in divorce courts. The no-fault dissolution of marriage acts sailing through state legislatures often are subject to a Women's Liberation provision. In Illinois, a new law directs the judge to regard maintenance as a temporary payment and consider the spouse's ability to find work or to acquire sufficient education or training to find appropriate employment. On the other hand, a landmark decision of the California Supreme Court may make the "wages of living in sin" as costly in this world as in the next. In granting a financial settlement to the ex-mistress of a Hollywood star, the court declared: "The mores of the society have indeed changed so radically in regard to cohabitation that we cannot impose a standard based on alleged moral considerations that have apparently been so widely abandoned by so many."[2]

Not all lawyers are enthusiastic about the ruling. "People

155

already go in and out of marriage like they go through a swinging door," said one West Coast attorney. "What makes this case ludicrous is that it completely strips all meaning out of getting married. There would no longer be a purpose for having rules and regulations for marriage. It would make a mockery of what we consider our basic social institutions."

Right on, Gloria Steinem! Several years ago she predicted, "For the sake of those who wish to live in equal partnership, we have to abolish and reform the institution of legal marriage."

Feminist "peace" initiatives also are making an impact. Britain's respected publication, *Jane's All the World's Aircraft,* projects that President Carter's decision to scrap the B-1 bomber may have cost us World War III. Said *Jane's,* "Soviet leaders must be surprised beyond belief that the U.S. president has disposed of the B-1 without asking any Soviet concession in return." One of the IWY resolutions passed in Illinois was to dump the strategic B-1 and use the money for women's projects.[3] And before Carter cancelled the neutron bomb, Ms. Costanza arranged a meeting between defense advisors and IWY commissioner Ethel Taylor who demanded it be quashed.

While Women's Lib works behind the scenes to restructure society, the Equal Rights Amendment remains out front as the cohesive spark. Initiated by NOW, the ERA boycott against convention cities in unratified states will hurt the very people proponents claim to champion—working women! Yet dozens of groups are falling in step: the American Association of University Women, the National Education Association, the League of Women Voters, and the Methodist and Presbyterian churches to name a few of the abetting organizations.

Yes, it is "Only the Beginning: A Blueprint for Equality," as the folder in our IWY delegates' packets reminded us. Published by the UN Association of the U.S.A., the leaflet was co-sponsored by AAUW, LWV, NEA, YWCA, National Federation of Business and Professional Women's Clubs, Population Crisis Committee, churches and others. Inside were our "Assignments for Action" to carry out the World

Plan adopted at Mexico City: Support the ERA, promote legislation to implement the provisions of IWY, review school curricula to eliminate sex stereotyping, support the National Women's Agenda. Equality is the guise; an ungodly world dictatorship is the goal!

My late friend, Dr. Nicholas Nyaradi, former finance minister of Hungary, escaped to freedom where he became head of the international relations department at Bradley University and an advisor to the U.S. State Department. He spent the rest of his life telling Americans, "We felt so sorry for poor Eastern Europeans but we, of course, knew it would never happen to us freedom-loving Hungarians. Don't ever believe that it can't happen here."

It doesn't have to. God's promise is at our disposal: "If my people, who are called by my name, shall humble themselves, and pray, and seek my face, and turn from their wicked ways, then will I hear from heaven, and will forgive their sin, and will heal their land" (II Chronicles 7:14).

To illustrate Christian responsibility, Nyaradi used to tell about the missionary who took his Bible and a gun into the jungle to preach the Gospel.

"But why," asked a colleague, "do you take a gun?"

"Because," the preacher answered wisely, "the tigers might not be able to read!"

Jesus enjoined us similarly: "Behold, I send you as sheep in the midst of wolves; therefore, be as shrewd as serpents and as innocent as doves" (Matthew 10:16).

Not long ago, Illinois State Senator Robert Mitchler reminded me that freedom is not free—it must be earned and preserved by each succeeding generation. So if you liked financing International Women's Year activities for the Women's Lib movement, you're going to *love* the International Year of the Child and the White House Conference on Families in 1979!

The choice is yours. Will you "walk in wisdom toward them that are outside, redeeming the time" (Col. 4:5), or will you pay the price of LIBerty?

Index

Notes

Chapter 1

1. Citizens' Advisory Council on the Status of Women, *Women in 1970* (Washington, D.C.: Government Printing Office, March 1971).

2. "Liberated Women: How They're Changing American Life," *U.S. News & World Report*, (May 7, 1976): p. 46-49.

3. George F. Gilder, *Sexual Suicide* (Bantam Books, 1975), p.162-163.

4. *REVOLUTION: tomorrow is NOW*, policy manual of National Organization for Women, national conference resolutions, (1973).

5. *National Plan of Action*, National Women's Conference, IWY Commission, P.O. Box 1567, Washington, D.C., (65¢).

6. "What Next for U.S. Women," *Time*, (December 5, 1977): p.25.

7. Robert S. Mendelsohn, "Can the American Family Survive?" *Peoria Journal Star*, (December 7, 1975): p. E-1.

8. "Survey Links Sexual Pleasure," *Ibid.*, (September 28, 1975).

Chapter 2

1. Francis A. Schaeffer, *How Should We Then Live?* (Fleming H. Revell, 1976).

2. "Abortions Hold Down Illinois Birth Rate," (AP), *Peoria Journal Star*, (November 28, 1977).

3. Diehl et al., *Health & Safety for You*, 4th ed. (McGraw-Hill Book Co., 1975), p.297.

4. "Women's Stake," *New York Times*, (April 30, 1972): Sec. 12.

5. "...To Form a More Perfect Union...." report of the National Commission on the Observance of International Women's Year, (1976): p. 271. Copies available from IWY, P.O. Box 1567, Washington, D.C. ($2).

6. Charles and Bonnie Remsberg, "Second Thoughts on Abortion from the Doctor Who Led the Crusade for It," *Good Housekeeping*, (March 1976): p.69.

Chapter 3

1. Casper Weinberger, "Growing Danger to Freedom," *Peoria Journal Star*, (August 10, 1975).

2. James C. Hefley, *Textbooks on Trial* (Victor Books, 1976). Questions on textbooks may be directed to The Mel Gablers, Educational Research Analysts, P.O. Box 7518, Longview, TX 75602.

3. Onalee McGraw, *Secular Humanism and the Schools: The Issue Whose Time Has Come* (The Heritage Foundation, 513 C. Street, N.E., Washington, D.C. 20002, 25¢).

4. *Congressional Record*, Vol. 123, No. 194 (December 7, 1977), p. S19425. Available from Sen. Jesse Helms, 411 Russell Bldg., Washington, D.C. 20510

5. Verne P. Kaub, *Communist Socialist Propaganda in American Schools* (1953), p. 110-111. Available from Laymen's Commission of the American Council of Christian Churches, P.O. Box 8775, Pittsburgh, PA.

6. *Humanist Manifestos I and II* (Buffalo, N.Y.: Prometheus Books, 1933, 1973). Available from bookstores and Association of the W's, P.O. Box 2324, Ft. Worth, TX 76101, $2.

7. John Steinbacker, *The Child Seducers* (Educator Publications, 1971), p.7.

Chapter 4

1. Onalee McGraw, *Secular Humanism and the Schools: The Issue Whose Time Has Come* (The Heritage Foundation).

2. Dunning et al., *Focus* Galaxyie Series (Scott Foresman Co., 1969), p. 67.

3. *Women of the Whole World—Journal of the Women's International Democratic Federation*, Vol. 2, (1977), p. 45-46.

Chapter 5

1. Phyllis Schlafly, *The Power of the Positive Woman* (Arlington House, 1977) p.136-137.

2. "Ohio Task Force Report for the Implementation of the Equal Rights Amendment," (July 1975), p.17-20.

3. "Unexpected Results of Washington State ERA," *Minneapolis Star,* (November 22, 1976).

4. "How ERA Changes State Support Laws," *Phyllis Schlafly Report* (April 1971). c/o STOP ERA/Eagle Forum, Box 618, Alton, IL 62002.

5. Sen. John A. Welborn, Michigan State Senate, press release (March 1, 1976).

6. Letter from office of The Director of Selective Service, Washington, D.C. 20435 (January 23, 1975).

Chapter 7

1. Paul Freund, *Harvard Civil Rights-Civil Liberties Law Review* (March 1971). (Quoted in *Phyllis Schlafly Report,* November 1972, p.2.)

2. Sylvia Porter, "Social Security Decision Tip on Things to Come," *Dayton Daily News* (April 9, 1975), p.28.

3. "Voice of the People—Assembly Line Sisters," *Chicago Tribune* (February 16, 1974).

4. "Women's Rights Add to Women's Risks," *Family Circle* (May 1975).

5. "3,000 March Down Fifth Avenue in International Women's Rally," (AP) *Peoria Journal Star* (March 9, 1975).

Chapter 8

1. Hanson W. Baldwin, "Putting Women in Foxholes Will Weaken Armed Forces," *Waterbury* (Conn.) *Sunday Republican* (March 28, 1976).

2. National Business & Professional Women's Club, *Who Will Defend America?*

3. "Salt II—Blueprint for Disaster," *Reader's Digest* (April 1978), p.89.

4. George Will, "What Happened to Bella Abzug?" *Atlanta Journal* (February 20, 1978).

5. "Bring Back the Draft?" *U.S. News & World Report* (February 14, 1977), p.55.

6. "Russia's 'Rentless' Arms Build-Up," *Ibid.,* (January 17, 1977), p.35.

Chapter 9

1. "News & Views," *Faith for the Family,* (March/April, 1976), p.24-25. Bob Jones University publication.

2. "Will ERA Force All Private Schools Coed?" *Phyllis Schlafly Report* (December 1976).

3. "Feminism Invading Religious Thought," *Tazewell Publications* (Morton, IL: March 17, 1977), p. 18.

4. Claudia Feldman, ' "Times Have Changed,' Says Gay Activist after Parley Vote," *Houston Chronicle,* (November 21, 1977), Sec. 1, p.12.

Chapter 11

1. *Dept. of State Bulletin,* United Nations Conference of the International Women's Year, (August 18, 1975).

2. Helvi L. Sipila, "Women & World Affairs," *Today's Education,* (November/December, 1974), p.66-67.

3. Noel F. Busch, "The Furor Over School Textbooks," *Reader's Digest,* (January 1976).

4. Testimony before ad hoc hearings on IWY (Jacqueline Sumner, Iowa), Russell Office Bldg., Washington, D.C., September 14-15, 1977. Available from Sen. Jesse Helms.

5. *Dept. of State Bulletin,* op.cit.

Chapter 12

1. *Congressional Record,* Vol. 123, No. 194, (December 7, 1977), p. S19425. Available from Sen. Jesse Helms.

2. Anne Brataas, "Women Panelists Examine Status of Women in China," *Peoria Journal Star,* (September 12, 1977), p.A-6.

3. *Federal Register,* Vol. 43, No. 67 (April 6, 1978).

4. Heidi Steffens, "Cuba: The Day Women Took Over Havana," *Ms.,* (June 1975).

5. Kate Millett, *Sexual Politics* (New York: Doubleday, 1970), p.126-127.

6. Arianna Stassinopoulos, *The Female Woman* (Random House), p.126-128.

Chapter 13

1. Resolution #434 against World Government, approved by 78th National Veterans of Foreign Wars Convention, 1977 (Originally approved 1972).

2. Mary Ellen Riddle, "World with Too Many People Result of Blessing That Backfired," (NEA) *Peoria Journal Star,* (September 23, 1969), p.A-4.

3. Edward Edelson, "A Computer Views Our Future with Alarm," *Book World (Chicago Tribune),* (March 26, 1972), p.13.

4. "Girl, 7, Center of Fight over Laetrile," (AP) *Peoria Journal Star,* (August 18, 1977).

Chapter 14

·1. James J. Kilpatrick, "Anti-Libbers on the Warpath," *Newsday,* (July 8, 1977).

2. National Educators Fellowship, P.O. Box 243, South Pasadena, CA 91030.

3. Bing Crosby, "Bing's Last Message: I'm No Loner," *Chicago Tribune,* (October 16, 1977), Sec. 1, p.19.

4. Sara Anderson, "Women vs. Women: Grabbing for Grassroots," *Worldwide Challenge,* (November, 1977), p.40-42. Campus Crusade for Christ publication.

Chapter 15

1. "Why Women's Lib Is in Trouble," *U.S. News & World Report,* (November 28, 1977), p.29-32.

Chapter 16

1. "Saunier Named to Post on HEW Advisory Panel," *Dayton Daily News,* (January 19, 1978).